To: Chris—

Keep 'em laughing!

SPEAKING *of* FUNNY

77 WAYS
TO ADD
HUMOR
TO ANY
PRESENTATION

David Glickman
with a FOREWORD *by* DAVE BARRY

First edition published under the title:
Punchline Your Bottom Line
Copyright © 2003 by David Glickman

Second edition, Revised, published under the title:
Speaking Of Funny
Copyright © 2018 by David Glickman

Publisher: BookBaby

ISBN (Print Edition): 978-1-54391-929-5
ISBN (eBook Edition): 978-1-54391-930-1

To order additional copies of this book, visit
www.SpeakingOfFunny.com

For more information on the author, visit
www.DavidGlickman.com and www.FunnierSpeeches.com

David Glickman, Inc.
7853 Gunn Highway, #393
Tampa, FL 33626
David@DavidGlickman.com

For My Parents
Louis & Debbie Glickman

Who made every night at the dinner table
memorable because of the laughter…

Acknowledgements

This book would not be possible without the help and support of a lot of people, too many to mention here. But I'll take a stab at it anyway.

Thanks

To Susan, my funny and supportive wife. Thanks for being the ultimate sounding board and cheerleader—not just for this book, but for every project I've undertaken in the last 25 years. You're the best partner in the world.

To my sons, Howard and Sam, who make me laugh and inspire me to do greater things on a daily basis.

To my Mom and Dad, to whom this book is dedicated. While they are no longer with us, but I'll always be eternally grateful of how supportive they were of my dream to make a living from laughter. I know they would be thrilled with this book.

To my brother, Bob, who has been my "go-to guy" for over thirty years for coming up with the perfect funny line whenever I'm stumped.

To my sisters, Betsy and Penny, who have always been much funnier than I've given them credit for. Really, you guys are funny.

To all my friends in the National Speakers Association, who have been so supportive and encouraging and enthusiastic about my career and projects like this. If I tried to name all of you, it would require several more pages—and I'd still probably forget a few people. (I was able to fit 28 of your names into a song during my *Speaker Hall of Fame* acceptance speech and it *still* wasn't enough!)

And to Dave Barry, for writing the Foreword, and giving this book "instant credibility." Thank you so much for lending your name and words to the project.

If your name on the cover helps convince just one person that they can be funny....just one.....well, then, it was probably a bad idea. I was kind of hoping for thousands!

Seriously, Dave, I value your friendship and I thank you for honoring me with the Foreword.

CONTENTS

Foreword
by
Dave Barry

David Glickman is funny. I mean really, really funny. He makes me laugh so hard that milk spurts from my nose — and I don't even drink milk. He's so funny he makes me hold my sides, thighs, and roll on the floor, crying and begging for mercy.

And that's just because of the way he looks. When he talks, he's even funnier.

I've known David for more than 25 years, as a friend and a fellow humor professional. For many years, we co-hosted a charity event in Miami, making idiots out of ourselves onstage for a good cause. That meant that every year I got to watch David blow the audience away with his brilliant stand-up comedy and hilarious parody songs. And every year I would think, *How does he do it?*

And now, lo and behold, David has written a book revealing how he does it, and how others can do it, too. This is a great service to humanity. The leading cause of mortality in America — especially corporate America — is audiences being bored to death by speakers.

Think about all the agonizingly tedious presentations you've sat through. Think about the banquets where you've had to stab yourself with your dessert fork to keep from passing out while listening to a speaker so dull that even the dead chicken on your plate was snoring.

You don't want to be that kind of speaker. Most people don't. But most people, including probably you, are afraid to try to be funny. You think you'll fail, and look stupid. So you go with safe, and boring. And nobody listens to you.

But guess what? Humor isn't really that hard. There are things that work, and things that don't work, and you can learn these things! David Glickman will teach you. And if you do what he says, you will be funny. Maybe not as funny as David: That would require plastic surgery. But funny enough to keep an audience's attention, so you can get your real point across. Funny enough that people will actually enjoy hearing you talk. Maybe even funny enough that, when you're done, you'll get a standing ovation, with the entire audience on its feet. Including the chicken.

Introduction

Thank you for taking the time to read this book that is marketed under the pretense that it will show you how to "add humor to any presentation." Actually, now that I've got your attention, I wanted to let you know about an incredible multi-level marketing opportunity that gives you the opportunity to make $25,000 a week, working from home. Just this week, this amazing business venture made over 1.3 million dollars for hundreds of families just like yours.

Wait, stop! Don't put the book down! It's a joke....I'm kidding. We really are going to go into depth on how to get laughs in any public speaking situation or business presentation. I just wanted to prove that sometimes a little thing like that can give you a chuckle.

Now, come on, admit it, you did smile once you realized it was a joke, didn't you? It's ok. We don't have to be afraid to laugh anymore.

There has been a decided paradigm shift since the start of the 21st century from humor often being thought of as "silly" or "not appropriate," to it being a welcome addition to practically every area of society. Even with the added scrutiny of political correctness, there has still been an incredible insurgence of humor into the heretofore "no humor permitted" corporate world.

Out-of-control stress in both work and home life swung the pendulum too far to one side. Humor is now being used as one of the most powerful forces to help swing the pendulum back to center. Humor plays an increasingly important role in today's society.

Humor sells.

Humor heals.

Humor breaks the ice.

Humor negates anger.

Humor creates credibility.

Humor gets votes.

Humor gets noticed.

NO FUNNY HATS!

This is *not* a book on "humor in the workplace." That's a whole different school of humor, usually along the lines of recommending that we "wear funny hats or red clown noses" to eliminate all problems at work. This book concentrates on how to use humor in *live presentations*—whether you're presenting to one person or to several thousand people—and leveraging those laughs for your gain.

This book was originally written with the title, "But I'm Not Funny!" The words "But I'm not funny!" are a very familiar cry to many people who are required to speak to audiences from time to time. Why even try to get laughs when you know you're going to make a fool of yourself?

Well, with this book in hand, you can't use the "But I'm not funny!" excuse any more. You'll have to come up with a new one. If you follow the tips in this book exactly as written, you will get laughs from any audience.

I speak from experience—I've used every one of these tips extensively—and continue to use them—with the consistent reward of laughter.

These tips are not based on theory; these tips are based on reality. After having spoken to several thousand audiences, I know what works. I know how to get laughs. And now, for the first time, I've decided to document these techniques—most of which are being revealed here for the first time anywhere in print.

I really want you to relax and enjoy the book, knowing that I've gone ahead and "road-tested" these tricks for you. I want you to feel confident to get out there and try them—and, most of all—to have fun!

Most of the 77 tricks, tips and techniques in this book are derived from the world of stand-up comedy. But don't worry, no one is expecting you to be a stand-up comic. As a matter of fact, a large part of your success will be because you're *not* a stand-up comic. You're *not* expected to be hilarious. And when you *are*, the audience reaction is that much stronger, because of the surprise element.

When a stand-up comic hits the stage, there is no room for error. He or she is being paid to get laughs, and must have the proper tools to get those laughs in any situation.

Here's the good news: Many of those same comedian's tools can work equally as well, if not better, for the business executive, the salesperson, the committee chairperson, the team leader, etc. When you *are* funny—it's a bonus, a treat, and gives you instant credibility with the group you are addressing.

If you can get your audience to laugh at something in your presentation, you gain instant credibility.

We do business with people we like.

We *like* people who can make us laugh.

And when people are laughing, they don't feel like they're being "sold."

And although this book is designed for getting laughs in a live situation, you can be inspired to expand your "humor horizons" in other ways. For example, I strongly recommend humorous outgoing voicemail messages.

It can be as simple as, "Hi, this is David Glickman. You've reached my voicemail, which means I'm not available right now. And, yes, it is a voicemail system. I assure you it's not an answering machine where I'm sitting here screening your calls. I wouldn't do something like that. That's what I've got Caller ID for. So please leave me a message and I will call you back as soon as I can." You know the person on the other end of the phone is smiling.

HUMOR BREAKS THE ICE

Many years ago I was asked to design a "comedy curriculum" for a traffic school. This is a "driver improvement" class for people who have received a traffic ticket. I can't think of a group of people who are more unhappy to be sitting in a room.

Many don't feel they deserved the ticket.

Most are angry.

And none of them are looking forward to sitting in a classroom for four hours.

I began the class by launching immediately into a song parody of the Warner Brothers "Looney Tunes" theme song:

This is it. Its traffic school. Don't feel bad. You're not a fool.
Almost everyone's breaking the law. But you're the one they caught.
I am Dave. This is your class. Four hours long.
A pain in the. . . (pause) But who knows what you'll learn.
On with the class, this is it.

[handwritten note: — Great song idea for an opening.]

The whole thing was less than thirty seconds, but it served its purpose. I caught them totally off guard, acknowledged the fact that they didn't want to be there, and got some instant laughs.

Did it change the fact that they had to be there for four hours? No! But what it *did* change was their approach to the whole experience. I then launched into the curriculum to a much more receptive crowd.

Using humor as an icebreaker makes difficult tasks a whole lot easier.

HUMOR DIFFUSES TENSION

A speaker is heading to the lectern, trips, and falls down. The crowd gasps and there is immediate tension. The speaker quickly looks up and says, "I will now take questions from the floor." A huge laugh follows, and the speaker picks himself up and regains his dignity. (See Tip #49 for more information on this technique.)

Not all of us can think that quickly on their feet....or off their feet, as it were. But when faced with a tense situation, the power of humor will work more quickly to diffuse it than any other remedy.

Another speaker steps onto the platform. Either the wood is rotted, or the supports are bad, but the speaker falls right through the platform, as it collapses around him. Again, tension fills the room. Until the speaker quickly looks up and says, "Don't mind me. It's just a stage I'm going through."

When I heard that story, I was so impressed with the speaker's quick thinking, I wanted to design a stage to collapse—just so that I could have the opportunity to use the line. (I wisely decided not to.)

Both of these stories illustrate how humorous quick thinking can not only diffuse tension, but can raise your credibility to an even higher level than had there been no problem.

During the presidential campaign of 1996, Bob Dole had a problem one day while making a campaign appearance. He was shaking hands from a slightly elevated area, behind a fence. At one point the fence gave way, and Dole tumbled forward and fell to the ground. It was a tense moment for all, and, luckily, he was not injured.

However, had Bob Dole thought to look up from the ground at that moment and say (loudly), "*Live, from New York, it's Saturday Night!*," he would have gotten a huge laugh, and would have shot up several points in the polls. I don't know whether it would have changed the election results, but I do know it would have given him some great momentum that he desperately needed at that point.

HUMOR GETS RESULTS

The bottom line is that humor gets results. When I was a child, I remember how my father would handle the times when I would get very angry. He would find ways to make me laugh. He understood the power of humor.

l remember going to him, very upset, and yelling. And I would try to resist his attempts to make me laugh— *"Don't do that, Dad! I can't stay mad when I'm laughing!"*

And he would say, "That's exactly right, David. You can't stay mad when you're laughing." And then in a few minutes we would talk about what was upsetting me....in a rational, calm manner.

l learned some important life lessons from that. Lessons that have given me the ability to make an entire career out of bringing that power of laughter to audiences and into organizations.

Sales and marketing people are hungry for any tools that will help them make more sales. Humor is that tool.

Business executives are grasping for tools to gain credibility with their employees—or their shareholders. Humor is that tool.

Managers in organizations are looking for ways to make their meetings exciting. Humor is that tool.

Professional speakers are striving for techniques to set them apart from their competitors and help them get more bookings. Humor is that tool.

Not the "two guys walk into a bar" kind of humor; but clever, relevant-to-the-situation, professional, perfect-for-a-Dilbert-cartoon kind of humor.   oh yes!!!

If you commit to using even a handful of the 77 techniques you're about to read, you will get many laughs and harness the power of humor. And you'll never have to utter the "But I'm not funny!" cry again.

77 WAYS
TO ADD
HUMOR
TO ANY
PRESENTATION

1

"And now here's someone who needs no introduction" —Yes, they do!

ANY TIME YOU ARE MAKING A PRESENTATION—EVEN if it's only to a few people—get someone to introduce you. Even if you have to recruit an audience member to do it, arrange with someone before you begin your presentation to do you the honors.

Have your introduction typed out, double-spaced in a large font. Often you are able to pre-arrange your introducer with enough lead-time so that you can send them your introduction long before the date of the presentation. (Of course, always bring a backup copy with you—the introducer may have forgotten it, lost it, or simply not shown up!)

Why do you want to be introduced if you're only addressing a group of ten people around a boardroom table? Because it sets the stage that you are, indeed, "presenting" to them—that this is not just another boring speech.

An introduction says "it's show time!" And if you're going to use some of the other 76 tips that follow this one, you must set the stage to "be funny." An introduction helps do that.

We've been conditioned to hear entertainers "being introduced." We've been conditioned to applaud as an introduction ends with the words, "Please welcome Joe Smith!" If you want to get an audience laughing, from now on you must think of yourself as an entertainer every time you address an audience—even a small audience.

An introduction should not be long. Actually, the shorter, the better. Honestly, nobody really cares about all of your awards and degrees and what you've written and what you've done. Even the aura of a celebrity wears off real fast if their presentation isn't entertaining. Audiences judge you solely on what comes out of your mouth—right now.

If the audience is talking, distracted, or milling around, the introducer should take as much time as needed to get everyone's attention, and get them settled, before beginning your introduction. This may take an extra minute or two, but it's well worth it! I've seen too many introducers just barrel through the speaker's intro, while the audience members were still standing and chatting with each other.

If you don't have the lead-time to pre-arrange your introducer (or your chosen introducer doesn't show up), ask someone at the event or meeting to do it for you. Try to pick someone who is well-known to the audience, as it lends credibility to the intro.

However, if your "pre-presentation radar" scans someone in the room who seems very upbeat and gregarious, they are usually another good choice. (Sometimes they are even a better choice, because the high profile person you select may be extremely dull when it comes to introducing you. However, a dull introduction is better than no introduction at all.)

A back-up plan is to have your introduction pre-recorded—by someone else, not you—and played from your computer or your phone. (A computer is typically going to have a better speaker, but a cell phone might be easier to use in the moment.) It's certainly not as effective as being introduced live, but a taped introduction is better than no introduction at all.

So, with that being said, ladies and gentleman, please welcome Tip #2!

2

Make the last line of your introduction a funny line

AN INTRODUCTION BRINGS YOU TO THE FRONT OF your audience with applause. Usually when people are applauding, they are also smiling. If you want to be perceived as funny, then you should also have them laughing when you are being introduced.

I know several business people who have written some funny lines into their introductions that get some good laughs. But you should save at least one laugh line—if not your best laugh line—for the very end of the intro.

As the introducer says the last line, the audience laughs, and the introducer says (*while* the audience is laughing), "Please welcome Joe Smith!" Joe walks to the front of the room to laughter. There is no better way to start a presentation than to have the audience laughing before you ever say a word!

One funny line l have used sporadically over the years is from an old stock comedy club bit. The introduction ends with, "And we have some good news to share with you, that is being announced for the first time here today. Just this last Wednesday, David signed his first contract with HBO. (*The audience typically applauds at this point.*) Yeah, it's a great deal. He pays $10 a month, and gets 'Game of Thrones' and tons of movies. (*Big laugh on this line.*) Please welcome David Glickman!"

This line works well for me, because I'm an entertainer and it's conceivable that l could have signed an HBO contract. You need to create a line that works well for *your* role. If you are a professional speaker, you could use a similar theme, ".....She just signed a book deal with Doubleday. (*Applause*) Yeah, she gets nine books for a dollar, and only has to buy three more. (*Laugh*) Please welcome Jane Jones!"

Now, of course, if you already are a successful published author, that line wouldn't work. So you create a line that fits you: "Jane's best-seller is now in its fifth printing. And they'll *keep* on printing it until they get it right. (*Laugh*) Please welcome Jane Jones."

If you are a salesperson making a presentation, the line could be, "And now here's a man who would never clone himself....because he's afraid he would have to split the commissions. (*Laugh*) Please welcome Gary Gordon!"

If you are a physician giving a talk, the line could be, "It has been said that she is one the most accomplished physicians in her field. Now let's meet the person who said it. (*Laugh*) Please welcome Dr. Susan Scott. "

Self-deprecating humor, like the ones in these examples, is the best and safest kind of humor to use. It doesn't take away any of your credibility. If anything, it enhances it— showing the audience you are not afraid to poke some fun at yourself—and immediately increases your likeability.

What is my funny line?

When you give the introducer your written introduction, you should ask them to rehearse it with you once out loud. Tell them there's a joke at the end of the intro, and you want to make sure they're comfortable with the delivery. The delivery on the laugh line is crucial. Ideally, that last line should be delivered without the introducer looking at the paper, but by using direct eye contact with the audience.

So, now you've been introduced—and you're walking on stage to big laughs.

3

Loud = "Wowed!"
—Always use a microphone

JUST LIKE AN INTRODUCTION SAYS "IT'S SHOW TIME!,"
a microphone definitely sets the stage (no pun intended) that something "special" is about to happen. Entertainers always use microphones. Chances are that our greatest LPM (Laughs Per Minute) experiences as an audience member have come from someone who was holding a microphone—in most cases, a professional comedian.

So when we see someone holding a microphone, we make the association that the person is going to entertain us. (Until they prove otherwise.) And assuming the person with the microphone doesn't burst into song, the next leap of logic is that they're going to make us laugh.

Certainly there are other professions (politicians, clergy, etc.) who use microphones. But the most successful members of those professions are also the ones who are the funniest in front of an audience. So, yes, they are entertainers, too...in a specialized way.

When someone speaks into a microphone, their voice is amplified. And, for some strange reason, the fact that their voice is louder than everyone else's in the room gives them enhanced credibility and authority.

I've seen comedians do the same routine *with* a microphone and *without* a microphone, and the contrast was amazing. When using the microphone, the audience laughs were much louder, more frequent, and more enthusiastic.

This theory even holds true with a very small audience. If you are in a position where you are presenting to six or more people, I would recommend that you use a microphone.

I'm serious.

You don't have to make a big deal out of the microphone—as a matter of fact, you'd be better off making it as unobtrusive as possible. But, again, the amplification of your voice commands attention you may not otherwise get. I don't mean amplification at rock concert volume, but at a level where you are louder than everybody else in the room.

I was once hired by a man to perform a customized comedy routine at his wife's 50th birthday party. This gentleman was very prominent in the community and was paying a large fee for me to entertain at this party.

I spoke to him at length, as I gathered up information about his wife for my routine. The event was being held at his palatial home, and I assumed there would be a sizeable crowd.

When I asked him how many guests would be attending, he said, "Oh, it's just the four of us," referring to his family.

After my initial silence, he asked, "Is that a problem?"

I said, "No, no problem."

I think he sensed my uneasiness and said, "I could invite some neighbors over, too."

I said, "Yeah, good idea. That would be great!"

We ended up with six people for the party.

And, yes, l used a microphone—as l entertained the six people sitting around the dining room table.

Did I need to use a microphone? Of course not. l could have whispered the show and they would have heard it. But the microphone gave me the credibility and "permission" to get laughs from them. And, frankly, I think the microphone made the difference between what could have been a disaster and what turned out to be a very good show.

4

A microphone in the hand is worth two on the lapel

WHEN YOU THINK OF A PROFESSIONAL COMEDIAN doing a routine, you think of someone holding a microphone in their hand. That is the "industry standard" for people who get paid to make us laugh.

As a presenter, you want every possible advantage to get the audience laughing. A hand-held mike ("mike" is short for "microphone"; an alternate spelling is 'mic' but I prefer the former) gives you that extra little advantage.

In addition to the benefit of the appearance, the handheld microphone gives you some additional advantages over a lavalier mike. (Note: A lavalier mike is a small mike that clips to your lapel, with a wire coming out of it that usually goes through your shirt or blouse, and then is attached to a small transmitting pack that is clipped to your waist. If you watch the guests on late-night talk shows, most of them are wearing lavalier mikes. A lavalier mike is also sometimes called a lapel mike.)

A punchline is called a punchline because you are supposed to *punch* it with your voice. Even though you may not be telling jokes, per se, you will still have punchlines—which could also be called laugh lines. This is the line at the end of the piece of material you are doing that gets the laugh. To maximize your laughs, you should *punch* that line into the microphone—in other words, say it slightly louder—and bring the mike closer to your mouth.

You can't do that with a lavalier mike. You could certainly say the line a little louder, but you wouldn't have the advantage of being able to say the line closer to the microphone, as you can with a hand-held. I've even seen speakers who had a lavalier mike, put their head down and try to say the punchline into their lapel. Nice try, but it just doesn't work that way.

Some people worry that they need both their hands free in order to conduct their presentation. Well, that's why there are microphone stands! You can get the same benefits from standing in front of a hand-held mike placed in a mike stand. Your hands are free and you can hold up anything you want, and you're still getting the visual and audio advantages of the hand-held mike.

If a mike stand is not available, or you have to move around a lot, you can learn how to hold the mike with one hand and your materials with the other. There are many seasoned speakers who work in this manner.

You may even want to invest in your own microphone and sound system. If you're making a small sales presentation, there's a good chance they're not going to have a microphone for you. Remember from the last tip, you don't want to make a big deal out of setting up and using the mike. There are small battery-powered sound systems available on the market that are easier and quicker to set up than changing a light bulb.

I'm often asked if there's an advantage to a cordless hand-held microphone over one with a cord. The only slight advantage is that you may have a little more freedom to move around with a cordless mike. And if you're someone who wants to go into the audience as part of your program, cordless mikes are certainly more "user-friendly" for that purpose.

Corded mikes have their advantages, too. First of all, they *look* more like a microphone that we would see a funny person using. Secondly, there is always some humor that can be mined from the cord itself. Whether it's tripping over it, holding it up like you're reading it as a ticker tape, pretending it's really thick dental floss (which we need to handle that dinner we just had), and so on, it becomes yet one more tool on stage that's available to you.

You should check out the microphone you're going to be using, as part of Tip #5.

5

Check out the setting or you'll be regretting

IF AT ALL POSSIBLE, GET INTO THE ROOM WHERE you'll be presenting before any of the audience has arrived. This gives you a chance to check out the microphone and deal with other logistics before you are being watched by your quick-to-judge audience. There are certain elements that make a room conducive for humor. In order of importance, here they are:

A. The speaker must be well miked.

See Tips #3 and #4.

B. The speaker must be well lit and seen.

If you are speaking after a dinner, and the room has been set to a low-light dinner level, you need to find a way to raise the lights during your program, so you can be seen. Sometimes that means turning up the houselights.

Also, you need to check for pillars, posts, and any other obstructions that might block audience members from seeing you. If faced with these obstacles, you need to either move those seats, or be prepared to move around a lot, so that you can be seen by everyone.

C. The audience must be immediately adjacent to the stage or speaking area.

The farther away you are from your audience, the more difficulty you will have in making your humor work. If you are speaking at a function where dancing follows your presentation, there is often a dance floor between you and the audience. This is what's known as a "comedy moat" and does its job well in keeping the laughs away.

If possible, ask to see a floor plan before the event, so that you can try to move the "comedy moat" to the back of the room.

D. The audience must be seated.

This might sound like a no-brainer, but you'd be surprised how many times speakers are faced with the unusual scenario of a standing audience.

Again, you want to replicate the feeling of a "show," and that means the audience is sitting and you are standing. If everybody is standing, it takes away a great deal of your credibility, and it is much harder for you to command attention. (Plus you'll never know if you got a standing ovation!)

E. All distractions must be eliminated or minimized.

These include phones, squeaky doors, latecomers entering in the front of the room (versus the rear doors that should be used once the presentation begins), etc. Even small things—like a flickering light bulb in the front of the room—can cause people to be distracted.

If you are speaking at a meal function, you should pre-arrange that all the wait staff leave the room during your program. There is nothing that kills a laugh line quicker than a clanging plate, or a waiter loudly asking, "Would you like some coffee?"

F. If your audience is over 100 (people, not age), you should be elevated on a stage or riser.

(If they are over 100 in age, you had better have done a really good microphone check!)

The riser need not be tall—even a 6" riser is better than none at all. A riser (or stage) is not just to help the audience see you. Just like the microphone, the riser is also telling the audience that "this is a show" and they're seeing something "special." It is another tool to help you get laughs.

With the exception of this last item—being elevated—all of the other elements apply to you, even if you are just presenting to a dozen people in a boardroom.

You still want to be miked.

You still want to be seen.

You still want your audience close to you.

You certainly want them seated.

Great points

You want anyone entering or leaving the room to do it from a rear door, away from your where you're presenting.

Paying attention to these items will help you have your best shot at getting maximum laughs.

G. Avoid presenting from behind a lectern

Many speakers like the "security blanket" of standing behind a lectern. If they're nervous, It gives them something to hold onto. It "protects" them and creates a comfortable barrier between them and the audience. *LECTERN*

However, it is *not* the most ideal situation for getting laughs.

Certainly many speakers have presented very funny programs from behind a lectern. But our goal in this book is to *maximize your laughs*. And to gain every advantage that you possibly can, you'll want to "work without the safety net" of the lectern.

A possible compromise is for you to begin your program behind the lectern, but after a few minutes move away from it and work the entire stage instead.

Fun fact: Most people mistakenly call a "lectern" a "podium." A "podium" is actually the riser you are standing on. The formal definition of "podium" is "a small platform on which a person may stand to be seen by an audience, as when making a speech or conducting an orchestra."

So, technically, you should avoid the "lectern", but gravitate towards the "podium."

6

The more people in the space, the slower your pace

WHEN YOU ARE DELIVERING HUMOR TO A SMALL crowd, the laughs are immediate...they surround you. When you are delivering humor to a large crowd, the laughs travel in a wave....from the front of the room to the back of the room. It's a very unsettling phenomenon, and can rattle you if you're not prepared for it.

It's important to pause appropriately between laugh lines, depending on the size of the audience. In a large venue, you will actually feel the laughs move to the back of the room, while the laughs in the front are dying down from the same line.

You should try not to "step on your laughs"—meaning that you should wait until the particular laugh has ended before moving onto your next line. But sometimes you have no choice, or your pauses would be interminable. (Some comedians use long pauses for great effect. However, if you're the CEO of the company, people get nervous if you pause too long)

You can help finesse the timing by starting your next line with a few words that aren't important to the next thought. Something like, "Am I right? Huh? It's true." Even if the folks in the back of the venue don't hear those words—because they're laughing—they haven't missed anything. And as you start your next important line, you've got the whole audience back listening to you again.

7

The more, the merrier

LAUGHTER IS CONTAGIOUS. IF YOU ARE GIVEN THE choice of presenting to just the CEO, or to the Executive Staff of ten *without* the CEO—go for the Executive Staff of ten.

If you are in sales, this may go against everything you have ever been taught. If you have the chance to meet one- on-one with the CEO, you're supposed to "go for it." But if you want to maximize the techniques in the book, you will gain far more credibility and likeability if you do your 'shtick' for the ten people.

We do business with people we like—and we like people who make us laugh. And you'll have a far easier time making ten people laugh, than making one person laugh. (With the net result being you now have *ten* people advocating your message to the one person who makes the decision.)

It's not that the humor is any funnier in front of the ten people. It's just that we feel more comfortable laughing out loud when we're with other people. If you watch a funny movie in a theater, there is loud and raucous laughter. If you watch that same movie at home by yourself, you normally won't laugh anywhere near as loud and as often as you would in a theater full of people.

Now, don't get me wrong. You can certainly use humor in a one-on-one situation. But if you want to leverage your humor for its best possible results, you should always opt for the bigger audience.

Once your audience is over 50 people, you're into more of a public speaking situation. An audience of over 50 people is more than enough people for getting good laughs from good material. Your advantage doesn't change much whether it's 100 people or 1000 people. The only thing that really changes with the larger groups is your timing. (See Tip #6)

Many readers of this book will be making presentations to small groups, so it's important to remember that when it comes to getting laughs—the more, the merrier.

8

Setting the stage for humor

THERE ARE SEVERAL FACTORS THAT WILL HAVE A great bearing on how your humor is received by the audience.

These are:

A. Time of Day.

Humor has a hard time connecting first thing in the morning. The audience's brains experience some kind of "snooze alarm" when it comes to connecting well with humor. Not to say it can't be done. I've presented scores of hilarious 8 am keynotes. But it *is* more difficult.

Late morning through lunch is a great time for humor to work. From 2 pm to 5 pm, you're in your most difficult timeframe for humor, when most people would prefer a nap.

You start to bring back your receptiveness around dinner, and maximize it in the evening. This is because most of us are used to laughing at humor in the evening, whether that be at a comedy club, at a television sitcom, or at the movies. Night time is show time!

However, there is a point of diminishing returns. If your audience has been awake and working all day, and the event is dragging on with other speeches, perhaps with awards, you may be facing an exhausted audience if you're beginning your remarks much later than 9:00 pm.

B. Alcohol

There used to be an old saying in the comedy clubs. The comedian would tell the audience: "The more you drink, the funnier I am." And that's true, to a point.

When an audience has had one or two drinks, it does loosen things up a little bit. However, if an event has had an open bar for three hours prior to your presentation, that does not make for an ideal audience. They become too unfocused for much of the humor to work.

My experience has shown much better results in getting laughter with a totally sober crowd than with one that has been drinking (even just a little).

C. Room temperature

If you can get your hands on the thermostat in the room, make it a little cooler. This keeps the audience more alert, and more receptive to humor. If the room is too warm, people get tired, and jokes don't go over well if your audience is sleeping!

D. Floor plan

If you have the choice between theater-style seating (chairs only) and classroom-style seating (tables and chairs), opt for theater-style seating. It's more intimate, it puts the audience closer to you, and closer to each other.

Rather than lining the rows up straight, line them up in a semi-circle, so that the audience is seeing each other a little to their sides. When they are seeing each other laughing, it inspires them to laugh as well.

E. Room Size

Let's say the room where you're speaking can hold 300 people, but there are only 50 people who will be attending your speech. You should try to close off sections of the room so that it doesn't look so cavernous. You can use room dividers, screens, trees—anything to make the room seem more intimate.

If you aren't able to section off the back of the room, you should at least try to get the extra chairs removed. Most business audiences avoid the front rows of any event. In keeping with the advice in Tip #5—trying to get the audience as close to you as possible—you stand your best chance of getting the audience in those front rows by removing the extra chairs.

9

Audience gender and age affect your laughs

A. Gender

All-female audiences are generally the most receptive to humor. All-male audiences are the most difficult to win over initially. Mixed audiences are usually fine, as long as they know each other.

If it's strictly a business situation, where the men and women in the audience don't know each other, both sexes become a little hesitant to laugh initially. We will spend a lot of time in this book strategizing material to open your program with, because once you've won over your audience initially, you can usually keep them entertained.

B. Age

Like above, an audience that is mixed age-wise is your most receptive. If you skew too far one way or another, it becomes more difficult. A very young audience has a short attention span, and unless you are very young too, your material may just not be as relevant to them as you would hope.

An older audience has a better attention span, but you also risk not connecting with them, if your material is too current.

And both very young and very old audiences have no qualms about walking out if they're not having a good time. At least with a mixed audience, you're usually getting good laughs from a cross-section of the audience most of the time.

10

Every audience takes on its own personality

AN AUDIENCE IS LIKE A 100-HEADED CREATURE. Although there are seemingly many different people sitting there, they actually become one entity in their general response to you. It's not planned—it just happens.

That is why a speaker can use the exact same humor with two different audiences and get two totally different reactions. The demographics and dynamics can be exactly the same, and somehow the crowd decides "what kind of crowd" they're going to be. It almost appears to be telepathic! If you've ever heard a comedian say "good crowd" or "rough crowd," he or she is referring to this 100-headed creature.

Sometimes you can predict what personality the audience is going to take on. There are certain indicators. if everyone is sitting quietly before the program, you can bet they're going to be pretty quiet in their response to your humor. (An interesting side note: Often you'll find members of these audiences will come up to you after a program and tell you "how hilarious" you were. And they'll tell you this with absolutely no sign of joy or pleasure on their face. You begin to wonder if they are "laugh-challenged.")

If your audience is very loud and talkative before your program, there's a good chance that audience is going to have a much better personality. However, none of these indicators are foolproof. An audience can turn on a dime if you say something to offend them. I've seen the 100-headed creature change personalities faster than a chameleon changing colors.

This tip should reassure you that if you are getting blank stares instead of huge laughs, it may not be you. It may just be that that particular audience decided—and the decision is usually made very early in the program—that they're not in much of a laughing-out-loud mood today. Don't take it personally! If you're genuinely funny, this is something you won't run across very often.

11

2% of the audience will hate you

EVEN IF YOU'RE PRESENTING TO AN AUDIENCE WHO seems to be laughing at all of your humor, there will be always a handful of people who will not laugh at anything you say.

Why? Because they hate you. They are offended by you. They find no humor in the subjects you are joking about.

We all know people like this. These are people who wake up in the morning and whose day is not complete until someone has offended them. Their existence is based on how miserable they are.

Don't let these people rattle you! Luckily, they make up a very small percentage of your audiences. But they will be there! (And sometimes they'll even make it their business to come up to you after your program and tell you exactly how you offended them.)

Understand them for who they are. They represent the polar opposite of what you're trying to do with your humor. Don't debate them on the merits of your humor. If challenged, simply say, "I'm sorry you feel that way. I'm glad that most everyone else seemed to enjoy it." And walk away. Don't get sucked into their negativity.

There's a wonderful scene in the movie "Mr. Saturday Night," which stars Billy Crystal as an "old school" comic. Crystal's character, Buddy Young, Jr., is performing at a Catskills resort. He is absolutely killing the audience— they are pounding the tables, tears are coming out of their eyes, they're trying to catch their breath.

After the show Buddy is livid. His brother asks why. He says that there was a guy sitting front and center who never laughed once all night. As a matter of fact, the guy looked disgusted throughout the entire comedy routine. Buddy didn't care that he had several hundred people laughing hysterically for an hour. He was more upset that there was one guy out there who found nothing funny.

The point is that this one guy will be in *your* audience, too. Accept it, embrace it, and maybe even make it a game to look for him while you're speaking. As long as you realize there will be people who hate you and your humor, you won't take it personally.

12

If the audience talks with an accent, so do you

IF THE AUDIENCE SOUNDS DIFFERENT TO YOU, THEN you sound different to the audience. You're both thinking, "Listen to that accent!"

Now don't misunderstand the title of this tip—I'm not suggesting that you then talk to them in their accent. (That would backfire badly.) I'm simply alerting you to be aware of what language(s) your audience speaks, and adjust accordingly.

In most cases, it just means slowing down your delivery. If the audience is having to translate your humor in their heads, from English to their native language, it slows things down a bit. And you may need to pause a little longer between laugh lines, to wait for them to "get it."

This speaks to a bigger issue: Humor that transcends international barriers. The vast majority of the tips in this book are designed to work with a domestic U.S. audience. They've been tested with

U.S. audiences and work well with them. They may not work well for people from other countries.

Different nationalities find different things funny, and, unfortunately, I am not an expert on humor for other countries. The few times I have spoken to international audiences, I have had a difficult time getting the usual results from the stuff that "works every time." The fact that your international audience speaks English does not guarantee that they will find your humor funny.

Unless you can research what kind of humor works with the nationality you're speaking to, I would refrain from using most of the methods in this book for an international audience. I'm not suggesting that you turn down those speaking or business opportunities, but I would use extreme caution with your humor choices in these cases. This book will help you get laughs when the audiences are predominantly American.

13

Humor & Music
—It's all show business

EVERYONE LOVES A "MUSICAL COMEDY." THE COMBI-
nation of those two forms of entertainment can generate millions of
dollars in ticket sales. Although you may not plan on using any music
whatsoever in your program, you do have the ability to include music
as part of the experience.

Good presenters have music playing as the audience enters
the room. It doesn't have to be loud. It just has to be upbeat....excit-
ing....setting a tone that something fun is about to happen. It can be
with lyrics or without. It can be Motown or it can be classical. It can
be Top 40 or it can be jazz. As long as the music has good energy,
the strategy will work.

As it gets closer to the time of your speech, the volume of
the music should be raised slightly. And as your introducer walks
on stage to introduce you, it should be raised quite a bit. (This also
helps gets everyone's attention.) The music then stops while you are
being introduced.

When the introducer finishes your introduction (hopefully with the laugh line from Tip #2), the music can be cranked up again for the few seconds it takes for you to walk to the microphone. It should be faded down when you get to the mike, so you can launch immediately into your first line.

You're basically looking for the same feeling you see on a late-night talk show when the guests are introduced, and enter as music is playing. Remember, you're a performer, you're putting on a show. You can have much success getting an audience laughing, when you set the stage with music. (See Tip #73 for more info on using music at meetings.)

14

Don't follow the memorial tribute

SOMETIMES YOU WILL BE THE ONLY PERSON SPEAK-
ing on a program, and that is probably the best scenario you could
hope for. Every time you add other presenters to the mix, you are
risking many things that could affect how your humor is received.

Even something as mundane as "housekeeping announcements" before you speak at a meeting can be the unintentional kiss
of death. (Or in this case, the "announcement of death.")

I have had to follow announcements of the recent death of
a beloved member of the association or staff. After a moment of
silence, it was time for my introduction. If dear departed Fred was
known and loved by everyone—and many of them are hearing of
his untimely departure here for the first time—you are going to be
facing a crowd that has just lost their willingness to laugh right now.
It really would be disrespectful to Fred, wouldn't it?

Check with whomever is in charge of the event. Find out what's
on the program before you. Even if there's no dismal announcement,

you may be following a speaker who will be sharing a very emotional story about how they overcame a serious illness. If that's the case, ask if there can be a short break before your program. Your humor will be much better received if it can stand on its own, or as much on its own as the program will allow.

If there is no way to avoid following a memorial tribute or something emotional, you may need to adjust your opening. One way to approach it is by saying something like, "I can see how beloved Fred was to all of you" or "That was a very moving and inspiring talk that Gloria gave about her recovery." And then say this, "I'm sure all of you will want to think about what you just heard, in your own way and in your own time. I know I will. It also makes us realize how important it is to enjoy life as much as we can. So now, as we move into this next program, I'd like you to switch gears and get ready for some fun. You have permission to laugh—as a matter fact, I encourage you to laugh—and enjoy our time together right now."

If you can have your introducer say that for you—instead of you having to do it—it's even more effective. But most of the time, the introducer will want nothing to do with the awkward transition from the "sad moment" to the "happy moment." You'll have to do all the heavy lifting.

15

"Mirror, mirror, on the wall, who's the funniest one of all?"

DISTRACTION IS THE ENEMY OF HUMOR. JUST AS YOU want to avoid the distractions mentioned in Tip #5, you also want to check *yourself* for distractions that you, personally, may be causing.

Take a quick peek into your phone's camera in selfie mode. Or carry a small pocket-sized mirror that you can take a quick glance into before you begin your presentation.

You should be as subtle as possible when doing this check. if you lay the phone or mirror flat on top of your notes, you'll probably be the only one who sees it. You want to be subtle, because the audience is observing (and judging) you even before you begin speaking.

Many of them know you're the speaker, and they watch you in the same way they would watch a celebrity (As the one about to take the mike, you *are* the celebrity for that event.) They watch you while you're eating, while you're mingling, and especially while you're being introduced. Hence, your mirror check should be subtle!

Then, once you've been introduced, you are really under the microscope. Your opening is crucial (See Tip #26), but your appearance is equally important. If you've got spinach in your teeth, a spot on your shirt, something sticking out of your pocket, the audience will initially focus on that. The focus will fade, but the damage will have been done.

While you still may give a good program, your laughs will be somewhat diluted, because the audience's focus has been somewhat diluted.

If you find yourself displaying a distraction that can't be corrected —whether just discovered at that moment (a run in a stocking) or one that you're aware of (your arm is in a cast), you should acknowledge it humorously early in the program. Because until you do, that is what most of the audience will be thinking about as they watch you!

16

"Two guys walk into a bar......
and nobody cares!"
—Don't rely on jokes

IF I HAD A DOLLAR FOR EVERY SPEAKER I'VE SEEN open their program with a "joke," and then just launch into their speech, I could retire a rich man. This book takes the bold stand that you should *not* tell jokes. Period. There are better and more innovative ways to get laughs—leave the jokes to the other speakers. You are better than that.

When I say "joke," I'm referring to the classic definition of a short narrative or story, told in the 3rd person. They usually start with "Two guys walk into a bar" or "A man goes to the doctor" or some other clue that you're about to hear a joke.

If you want to tell a story that's going to get a laugh, tell a true one about yourself. Don't just switch the joke from "A man goes to the doctor" to "I went to the doctor." That's even worse. It's still a joke.

Why avoid jokes? First of all, most people don't tell them well. There's nothing worse than a poorly told joke.

Second, many jokes are offensive. While you may think the joke you've selected is fine, our hypersensitive society is more primed to be "offended by a joke" than almost any other type of humor you may use.

Also, jokes are widely told, so they're widely known.

There's a good chance that many of the members of your audience have heard your opening joke, too.

Now I'm not saying that the audience won't laugh at it. Good jokes—even old ones—if told well, *do* get laughs. I'm suggesting that joke telling is an "old school" way of getting laughs. If you want to break the boring cycle of bad humor, use the techniques in this book instead.

No Jokes – most people fail saying them
– many jokes are offensive
– they are widely told and known
Tell stories about yourself

17

However, if you must tell a joke......

OK, I KNOW SOME OF YOU LOVE JOKES, HAVE HAD great success with jokes, and will continue to tell jokes. And some of you will be hesitant to try some of the new techniques in this book, but have no hesitation in using a joke in your speech. If you insist on telling a joke (or jokes), here are a few suggestions to help you.

First of all, have confidence in your joke. You should test it on a few people first, to make sure it gets the laughter you're expecting. If you are hesitant about the joke working, the audience will definitely pick up on that. Audiences are like horses: they can smell fear.

When you tell the joke, don't rush! If you're nervous about the joke, you tend to speed up your delivery. This hurts the joke, and your nervousness becomes a self-fulfilling prophecy.

The best way to minimize any nervousness is to practice the joke.

Out loud.

Many times.

Over and over and over and over again.

And then another few times.

Have l mentioned practicing out loud?

A good joke without good delivery will sink you every time. (See Tip #24).

The punchline is the payoff for the audience. When you get to the punchline, take a half-second pause.

Look right at the audience.

Raise the level of your voice a little bit.

Lean into the microphone. (It's hand-held, right? See Tip #4)

And then say the punchline.

After you say the it, give the audience time to laugh. If the laugh is short, count quickly (to yourself) 2-3-4, and move on to the next line.

If the laugh is long, wait until you hear it starting to fade (which could be upwards of twenty seconds or more if it's a killer punchline), quickly count 2-3-4, and move on.

Be sure to adjust your timing if the length of the laugh is based on the size of the audience—See Tip #6.

One important thing to consider when selecting a joke—The longer the joke is, the funnier the punchline had better be! The longer the audience is sitting there hearing you build toward the punchline, the more their anticipation grows. Sometimes the audience even begins to snicker before you've gotten there, because they're so anxious. If the punchline doesn't warrant the big buildup, you will get a half-hearted laugh, coupled with some mild irritation.

Also, if you're going to tell a joke, do not think you are being clever by inserting the name of a high-profile audience member into the story. ("There's three guys on a plane. The Pope, the President, and our CEO Jack Jenkins.") It's an amateur technique that kills the joke from the beginning, because everyone knows that Jack Jenkins was not on a plane with the Pope and the President....and everyone knows you're now "telling a joke." It's an overused gimmick that the best humorists know to stay away from.

Big No No

18

Don't laugh at your own humor

THERE ARE MIXED SCHOOLS OF THOUGHT ON THIS, but I believe it's better to *not* laugh at your own material. Most professional comedians keep a straight face while they're getting gales of laughter. If their "character" is delivering a humorous observation about being upset at something, it adds to the laughter that the comic continues to appear upset. If he or she were to start laughing, it would break the magic.

Most of you reading this have no desire to be a professional comedian. And you're not portraying a "character" while you're speaking. But, actually, you are. You're portraying "you." And unless you're the type of person who goes around laughing all the time, you shouldn't do it during your program.

Certainly, you can smile—which is acknowledging that your audience is amused. But leave the laughing to them. You will make much more of an impact by *not* laughing at your material (while your audience is), than if you were to join them in the laughter.

The one exception to this is if you get a laugh on something you say spontaneously. In this instance, both the audience and you are being entertained by this line for the first time. You can even follow your collective laughter by saying, "Somebody write that down. I may use that again." Or "Wow! I'm doing stuff I haven't even written yet." Either way, you're permitted to laugh at something that happens "in the moment." The audience feels that they are in on "something special."

19

Don't try to be funny outdoors

I LOVE THE OUTDOORS. IT'S GREAT FOR BIKING, THE beach, sunsets, carnivals, etc. However, it's the pits for getting laughs! If your presentation is scheduled for outdoors, abandon most of the humor! Just get through it, without trying too hard to be funny.

Certainly, if you use some of the tips in this book, you will likely get some laughs. But chances are you will find much of your humor falling flat. If you think there are distractions *inside* a room, you can't begin to know how much there is to distract an audience when they're *outside*!

And because "the sky's the limit" (translation: there's no ceiling), the sound of laughs are not contained. That means that no one can hear the laughter well—it basically just dissipates. And if people don't hear other people laughing, they are much more hesitant to laugh. They may not even be aware that you're up there speaking, let alone trying to be funny.

Bottom line: The outdoors is for the beach, not a speech.

Good to know

20

Avoid political humor

I MIGHT HAVE JUST CALLED THIS, "DON'T RISK ALIEN-
ating some of your audience." When you do political humor, you
usually get laughs from the people who agree with your politics.
(And the audience does assume it's *your* politics, even if you're just
using the material to get laughs.) But you definitely put off the people
who aren't on the same side.

Even if you're speaking to an audience whom you think is predominantly of one political leaning or another, there will be people
in that audience who are on the other side. Unless you're specifically
speaking at a political event for that political party, you need to avoid
the political humor.

I've sat in many audiences of wonderful speakers who killed
their credibility (and likeability) with me, when they made jokes at
the expense of a politician or party that I may favor. I could tell from
the crowd reaction that I was in the minority. But if our goal is to get
laughs from a diverse audience, we need to show extra caution in the
humor we choose.

Some might argue that the late-night talk show hosts do plenty of political humor. That's true, but the late-night entertainers are making jokes strictly for the purposes of entertainment. You are not. Your speech or presentation is typically for a work-related reason. Politics and work don't mix. This book is geared to help you be more funny within the context of what you're already talking about.

So save the political jokes for the neighborhood barbeque. (And even then, you may risk alienating your neighbors. People get real funny about politics—no pun intended. Don't say I didn't warn you!)

No political Jokes... period.

21

"Mingle well, mingle well, mingle all the way."

THIS IS THE FIRST LINE OF A SONG PARODY I OFTEN perform to the tune of "Jingle Bells." The song makes a point about how important it is to mingle (aka "schmooze") in a business environment.

This also holds true if you are going to be making a presentation. If logistics allow, you should mingle with the crowd beforehand. Ideally, you've already been in the room before the audience. (Tip #5) Now it's time to get to know some of your audience members.

They're usually happy to meet "the speaker" before you begin your program. And when you begin, the people you've met are "instant allies." They're much more receptive to your humor, because they've already met you.....you're their "friend."

Some presenters feel strongly about *not* mingling before their program. They feel that it takes away some of their "power".... takes away from their mystique. While that may be true for some celebrities, those folks are probably not trying to get laughs from the audience. You are. You want to help get your laughs using any methods possible. Well, this method definitely helps.

The mingling also gives you the possibility of throwing some spontaneous humor into your program. If you find out something that's funny while you're chatting—or learn something that can be made into a funny line—you can then reference the person you met and get a laugh with the impromptu line.

So even if you don't like mingling, just fake it. When it comes time for you to step up to the microphone, you'll be glad you did.

And even though you mingle with the audience before your presentation, you should *still* have someone introduce you. (Tip #1) The combination of your introduction with your pre-program mingling greatly increases the chances for your humor to work.

22

Watch the speakers who present before you

THERE'S NOTHING WORSE THAN DOING A FUNNY line—one that always works for you—and hearing silence. You're baffled. And the reason for the silence may be as close as the speaker the audience heard right before you.

If you're still relying on jokes in your program (Tip #16), this is always a big risk. You don't know if the speaker before you told the same joke you're about to tell. You should try to watch as many of the speakers as possible that are presenting before you.

Sometimes it's not possible. For example, if it's a four- day event and you're speaking on the last day. That's why the more original humor and more customized humor you can use reduces the risk of repeating something that already got a laugh.

Occasionally, repeating a line can work in your favor, albeit unintentionally. You end up with a callback (Tip # 50) and don't even know it until you hear the laugh.

But most of the time it *doesn't* work in your favor. The audience hears something they heard earlier that day, and they just don't laugh. Or don't laugh as loudly. If it's a line that always gets howls, you might even ask the crowd, "Have you heard these before?" Whether they have or haven't, the question usually gets a laugh.

Watching the other speakers who present before you also gives you the ability to gauge the audience. This can be helpful if you pick up on what they're receptive to and their general state of mind. (Or lack thereof.)

Of course, if you're the first speaker at an event, this all becomes a moot point. But don't be surprised if the other speakers are watching you!

23

Knowing what's genuinely funny

AS YOU PUT TOGETHER YOUR HUMOR, HOW DO YOU know what's genuinely funny? Is there a "humor litmus test" for material? Yes. It's called "the audience." They will let you know what's funny.

Here's an important distinction. I define "the audience" as a "group of strangers." Not your family. Not your friends. Family and friends know you intimately and will laugh at things you say that strangers would stare at blank-faced. You have to design your humor so that a group of strangers find it funny.

If your audience are co-workers or people who report to you, that is kind of a middle ground. You are not a total stranger to them—and they may already like you. But it's a different dynamic than the reaction you'd likely get from family members and friends outside of work. You still need to be "genuinely funny" with work colleagues, because they're not going to laugh at you unconditionally.

Many speakers think that the strangers will start laughing once the speaker "grows on them." They think, "Hey, I'm likeable. Heck, I'm the life of the party. Once these people get to know me a little bit, they'll see just how funny I am."

The challenge in most business presentations is that there isn't time for the speaker to "grow on you." Funny is funny from the outset. If it takes 20 minutes for them to know you're funny, but you've only got 15 minutes to make your presentation, you're out of luck!

Another distinction of what's funny is that the audience is laughing honestly, and not because they are uncomfortable. This is also called a "nervous laugh." Sometimes a presenter will think their humor is connecting well, but the laughter they're hearing is really based on tension or embarrassment. This is usually reserved for the speaker who tries to use inappropriate humor or off-color jokes. Don't confuse nervous laughter with genuine laughter.

And genuinely funny humor does not need an explanation or a disclaimer of "well, you had to be there." It stands on its own.

The more you engage these humor techniques, the easier it will become to get any audience laughing. There is a definite learning curve when it comes to getting laughs. I've included this tip because it's imperative for you to understand that "funny" is only "funny" when it's funny to strangers.

24

The recipe of Material, Delivery, and Improvisation

THOSE WHO HAVE THE MOST SUCCESS IN GETTING an audience laughing strive to have the three ingredients necessary for this recipe.

They are:

1. Good material.

2. Good delivery.

3. Good improvisational skills.

By good material, I mean "planned" or "written" material that is funny. Material that you have worked on, created, prepared, or even purchased. Material that is well written and when delivered well, will get laughs.

Good delivery is the vehicle through which the good material is successful. You must inherently feel the timing in a funny piece of material. You must know which word to punch in a punchline. You must be able to show an appropriate range of emotion in your voice. Without the ability to give good comic delivery, the best-written piece of humor will just fall flat.

Additionally, you must be able to think quickly on your feet. You need to have the ability to go outside of your script, and come up with a funny ad-lib when something out of the ordinary happens during your program.

This recipe for success requires all three ingredients. Two out of the three will not cut it. It doesn't matter how good your material is, or how adeptly you can ad-lib, if your delivery is horrendous. We've all seen people try to tell a joke and botch it terribly. Most audiences have very little patience for a speaker with poor delivery.

And if you have good material and good delivery, but can't ad-lib your way out of a paper bag, you will likely fail. Improvisation is probably the one ingredient that many speakers don't realize they must have, too. You can have the greatest speech in the world, with a delivery that wins you awards every time. But if you can't "think funny" when it counts, you can count yourself out.

Unexpected stuff happens in front of audiences, and you have to be able to display the same wit you've been showing up to now in your program, or you lose credibility instantly

Luckily, there are ways to help you get better at all three of these ingredients. Most major cities offer classes in improvisational comedy. This is a great way to learn how to think quickly and be funny on your feet.

As far as humorous material, there are plenty of comedy and humor writers available to help you. (I'm one of them—feel free to contact me!) Many of these same writers can help coach you on delivery, too.

So make sure you've included all three ingredients in your recipe before you step up to the microphone. You'll get a much better "taste" of how to get an audience laughing.

25

"I've Gotta Be Me!"

THERE ARE GOING TO BE SOME TIPS AND IDEAS IN this book you may not feel comfortable doing. If so—*don't do them*! You must have absolute and total faith in your material. You must feel confident that it's funny—and that it's going to get laughs. If *you* don't have faith in your material, your *audience* won't.

As you begin to inject more humor into your programs—and you get big laughs—you will build your confidence to try more things that you would have previously steered clear of. Just like you develop a "learning curve" with most new skills, you also develop a "comedy curve" for knowing what humor will work the best for you.

However, there are certain things you may never feel comfortable with. For example, Tip #73 talks about having a hidden costume underneath your clothing—which you reveal as a surprise. No matter how comfortable you get with your new humor, you may *never* find that particular piece of material funny. If you don't think it's genuinely funny, you will deliver it with less than 100% dedication—and the material will suffer.

Most successful comedians have a stage persona that is pretty similar to their off-stage personality. That is one of the reasons they are so successful. They are not acting—they are just doing funny material loosely based on "themselves."

Of course, some humorists have a Jekyll and Hyde personality on-stage and off-stage, but they are totally confident with the on-stage "character" they are displaying. However, that won't work for most business presentations. In a work setting, it is important that you are as close to "you" during your presentation as possible. The humor you do must fit *your* style, *your* personality, and *your* demeanor, in order for it be the most credible.

26

How you begin is the
most important thing

WHEN YOU BEGIN YOUR PRESENTATION, <u>YOUR GOAL</u> should be to get a laugh within the first fifteen seconds! That's right—the first fifteen seconds. If you truly want to get an audience laughing, then <u>you must establish your ability to get laughs—instantly.</u>

If you've begun using the techniques in this book, you've been hopefully developing a reputation for being funny when you step up to the microphone. And with that reputation comes an expectation from your audience.

This is actually a good thing, as the audience is primed to laugh, and is more open to the possibility that what you will say will be funny. You still need to develop your material so that a room full of total strangers would laugh at it. (Tip # 23) But the more you can build a reputation *beforehand* that your presentations are usually funny, the easier time you will have in winning over an audience.

When you find yourself in a situation where you are a total unknown to the audience—and you don't have a "reputation" to give you an advantage—there are other things you can do to help yourself.

A good place to start is by implementing Tip #2—Make the last line of your introduction a funny line.

In addition to that, you can prepare audience handouts to be distributed before your talk that say something along the lines of "John Jones is known for his insightful and humorous look at the world of auditing." This helps posture you as a funny person before you ever open your mouth. You can ask that similar verbiage be placed on any pre-event promotional materials or on the agenda

Even with a "reputation" to assist you, you still must get that first laugh in the first fifteen seconds. Why? To establish credibility. To prove to the audience that you are funny. (Or are "still" funny, if they've already seen you in action.) To set the tone for what is to follow.

Think of your presentation as a roller coaster ride. Your reputation, your printed program description, your introduction—those are all elements of that initial slow steep ride up to the top of the track for your audience. That's the time for the audience's anticipation. When you first take the microphone, what comes out of your mouth should be that first joyous rapid-fire descent into laughter for the audience, as the roller coaster begins its journey around the track.

Once you've established that first laugh, the journey can take all kinds of twists and turns—including areas of the program where you *don't* want to be funny. Your audience will accept that.

Your less humorous content should be smack in the middle of the program. Or it can be scattered throughout the program. But you must open funny and close funny (with the priority in that order) to convince them you are, indeed, funny.

When comedian jack Benny would prepare his weekly television program, he would often spend more time working on the opening of the show than he would on the rest of the entire program. He knew how important it was to begin properly.

And lest you wonder how to get that first laugh in the first fifteen seconds, Tips #28 - #40 will give you many easy examples of how to do just that.

27

Don't ask them to "give themselves a hand" or shout "good morning."

THERE IS NOTHING THAT SCREAMS "AMATEUR" MORE than asking an audience to "give yourselves a hand for being here today" or shout "good morning" back at you. This is what I call the "cheerleader" method of beginning a presentation. In the hopes of generating excitement, many presenters use this technique, because they have seen others use this technique, and its use just keeps spreading like a bad case of lice.

Yes, the audience will probably follow your request and applaud or shout, out of politeness.

And they'll even probably shout it louder when you say, "Oh, we can do better than that—let's try it again: Good *Morning!*"

But the smiles on their faces are tired and the clapping is lackluster. Tempting as these lines may be, because they are so easy to do, don't fall into the trap of thinking these are acceptable methods to start things off. Any laughs you get from these hackneyed displays are not genuine. (See Tip #23)

If you're looking to "wake up" a crowd, do it with funny lines, (See Tips #28-40 for examples) If your reason for wanting to open with the "cheerleader" method is because the crowd is not paying attention or appears to be distracted, use other methods to get them focused before you begin: Raise the level of the music louder, shut off the lights, raise the lights, blink the lights, have your introducer take the necessary time to get them focused—there are many things that can be done to get the crowd ready for your presentation.

An exception to the "asking for applause" ban: If you use audience volunteers for anything during your program, it is acceptable (and encouraged) to ask for "a round of applause" for them when they have finished their participation. That applause is warranted for a specific activity done "above and beyond" the normally passive role of being an audience member. It does not fall into the same categories of "a round of applause" just for being there, or "a round of applause" for being a great crowd, which are not warranted.

28

The "Car in the parking lot" opening

THIS IS ONE OF THE EASIEST OPENINGS TO USE. WHEN you are introduced, you walk up to the microphone holding a piece of paper.

You say:

"Before I begin, I have a quick announcement. Apparently, (*looking at paper*) there is a car parked in front of the building (or hotel, etc.). It is a green 1997 Dodge Neon. (*looking back up again*) There's nothing wrong with it, but it's making the place look like *hell*. So if you could move it, they'd appreciate it."

Stupid, yes. Simple, yes. Does it work every time, Yes!

A few notes:

A. There may be times and events where it is inappropriate to use the word "hell." You can replace it with "but it's making the place look *terrible*." It will still get the laugh, although "hell" gets the bigger laugh.

B. If all (or most) of your audience flew to the event, don't use the opening. (They would not have a car parked there!)

C. Instead of the word "announcement" you can say "piece of housekeeping business," if it seems more appropriate. You can even reference back to your introducer and say, "l don't know why they're having me do this." Or "I guess they couldn't get this to you." Look befuddled, as though you're just seeing the paper for the first time, and are feeling a little awkward at having to make the announcement.

D. Always pick a model year that's about 20 years old. If, however, your audience is primarily driving older cars, go back about 30 years—you'll still get the laugh.

Funny approach to break the ice.

29

The "This is the largest crowd" opening

THIS IS AN OPENING TO USE IF YOU HAVE VERY FEW people in your audience. It's a great opening, because there are two laughs built into it.

You say:

"I must begin by telling you that I'm a little nervous up here. You see, this is the *largest* crowd I've ever spoken to. (*gets your first laugh*) No, I'm kidding. It doesn't matter. I do the same program for *25* people as I would for *2500* people. It's the same. So, in closing, I'd like to say, 'Thank you and good night'." (*put down the mike and walk away quickly, as the second laugh begins. Then turn around, come back to the mike, and begin again.*)

A few notes:

A. I've found this opening will work if there are less than 30 people in the audience. Once you're beyond 30 people, they don't consider themselves to be a small audience. The exception to that: If there are 50 people sitting in a room where there are chairs set for several hundred, you're back in the ball game.

B. Try to use the exact number of people in the room—and then have your second number be a number that's 100 times the first number. ("I do the same program for 13 people as I would for 1300 people.")

C. If you are so new at presenting that this crowd *is* the largest you've ever spoken to, then the joke will not work. You must be a fairly seasoned speaker (or give the appearance that you are) for this to get the laughs.

Not sure about using this one especially the walking away bit.

30

The "Under the pretense" opening

THIS IS ANOTHER EASY OPENING. YOU SAY:

"Thank you for that nice introduction. It's a pleasure to be here under the *pretense* that I will be speaking about our new product line (*or whatever your program is titled or about*). Actually, ladies & gentlemen, I represent a company called *Amway*. And I would like to talk to you all for maybe fifteen or twenty minutes about ......(*at this point, the laugh has built, and you just let the sentence drop all.*) No, I'm kidding. We truly are here to talk about our new product line."

A few notes:

A. When you do the first line, really emphasize the word "pretense."

B. After you have hit the word "Amway," you will often see several audience members glancing at one person in the crowd to gauge that person's reaction. This typically means the person they're looking at *is* an Amway dealer. You can play off of that and then ask the person if they're an

Amway dealer.

If they say "yes," you say: "Well, looks like we've got our-selves a turf war here."

If they say "no," you say, "Well, good, I hate splitting my profits." And then you move into the "No, I'm kidding..." lines and back into your program.

C. This opening works better if the audience doesn't already know you. For example, if you're addressing a group of your employees—who *know* you don't sell Amway—it doesn't get a very big laugh.

D. If you're ever speaking at an Amway convention, don't use this opening!

(If you were paying attention, you'll remember I used a variation on this technique to begin the book. You'll find that many of the techniques in the book can be tweaked or modified to create additional ways to get laughs.)

Interesting concept

31

The "We're here for three hours" opening

THIS OPENING REQUIRES A SMALL AMOUNT OF research to pull off. You want to find out the name of a nearby town that is perceived as being a "culturally backwards, redneck, stupid" (you get the idea) town. Sometimes, it can just be the smallest town in the area—which by its very nature of being small also appears to be "backwards."

Once you have come up with your name (for our example, we'll call it "Seffner"), you say:

"It's great to be here at this event, which will last for three hours. Three hours! Or. if you're from Seffner, that's (*stomp your foot three times on the floor—this is your first laugh*).

Oh, do we have some folks here from Seffner? Because I can talk slower. (*second laugh*)

A few notes:

A. This opening works best if you have a wooden floor or stage to stomp your foot on. If you don't, you must hit the microphone with your hand—while stomping on the floor—to give the effect as though your foot is making the sound. Your audience is paying attention to your foot, and doesn't usually realize you're making the stomping sound with the mike.

B. When doing your research, ask several people for the name of the "stupid" area. Get a consensus. If you go with just one person's opinion, you risk them not picking an area that will get the laugh.

C. Make sure that there will be no audience members—or very, very few—from the "stupid" area. This is imperative! The line may bomb if you have a lot of folks from that area in your audience.

D. Also make sure that the town or area that you select isn't one that is predominantly populated by any one ethnic or racial minority. The area needs to be fairly diverse, or, at the very least, not one that has a minority as its majority. Again, sometimes just naming the smallest town in the area will do the trick.

E. When given a choice of several equally "stupid" towns, pick the one with the funniest-sounding name. Some names just inherently sound funny.

F. If your audience is not from the local area, this opening will not work. They must be familiar with the area you're making reference to. You can sometimes substitute a national reference, if there's something going on in the news that is making that town look backwards. But a local reference is always much funnier.

G. The area you pick does not have to specifically be a town. It can be a county or other local area, as long as it gets the audience recognition that it's "stupid."

You can also use the name of a group of people who might be considered "stupid." For example, the line "And if we have any data security folks here from Equifax......" would work well at the time this book is being written. There will always be high-profile groups in the news that can lit into the "dim-witted" category. However, given the choice, the geographic reference works better than the topical reference.

H. You want your number of stomps to be at least three and no more than six. If the event is less than three hours or more than six hours, there are other options you can use. You can sometimes use the number of days the event is going on, the number of speakers that are on the program, the number of years this event has been going on—anything you can come up with that's going to give you between three and six stomps.

32

The "By a show of hands" opening

THIS IS ONE OF THE BEST OPENINGS FOR GETTING A laugh, but it involves some practice to get the timing just right. You say something like:

"By a show of hands, how many of you in the audience have been in your current jobs for at least ten years (*pause ever so briefly as the hands start to go up*) .... ..and are miserable?" VERY FUNNY

A few notes:

A. The key to making this work is to say the second half of the sentence just as the hands are going up in the air. Then you act surprised and say something to the effect of, "I had no idea!"

B. You can make this opening work with almost anything that relates to your topic or the event. You could say, "By a show of hands, how many of you attended this meeting last year .... ..and hated it?" Or, "By a show of hands, how many of you flew in yesterday ......but would have much rather stayed home?"

Good one

C. The first half of the question must be something that is not controversial and something that would cause no one to hesitate in raising their hand.

↑
Great points

VERY interesting
way to open.

33

The "Fake handout" opening

THIS OPENING WORKS BEST IF YOUR AUDIENCE IS less than 50 people. You create a "fake handout" that is sitting at everyone's chair or table before they enter the room. The "fake handout" should be related to the topic you will be speaking about, but be incredibly technical, long, tedious, boring; basically causing angst in the attendees who look at it while waiting for the program to begin. It can also be a "fake agenda" for the meeting you're about to chair. You begin by saying:

"I hope you've all had a moment to look at the handout in front of you. I'm sure most of you are thinking,

'Wow, this looks pretty exciting.' (*first laugh*)

No, truth be told, most of you are probably looking at it, thinking 'This is gonna be really bad.' Well, let me help you diffuse some of that frustration you may be feeling. I want you to pick up that handout and crumple it into a ball like this. (*You demonstrate with your copy; second laugh*) Go ahead—everyone do it!

Now, I want you to get that frustration out of your system, and give you a chance to get back at me for pulling this joke on you. At the count of three, I want you to go ahead and release that tension—and any tension you're feeling about being here—and pelt me with the paper balls. Ready: One, two three!" (*They throw the papers, third laugh occurs*)

A few notes:

A. Certainly you can see why this should be for a crowd of 50 or less. When you have a bigger audience, the papers don't all hit the front of the room; instead they often hit other members of the audience. Because it's just paper, there's no real harm done if that happens—but it's much funnier if all the balls hit you.

B. You probably want to avoid this opening if your program is on "Violence in the Workplace" or something along those lines. Use your judgment on whether this is an appropriate opening for your topic.

C. If you have a real handout you'll be using, you can pass it out immediately *following* the ball toss. Remind your audience (for a fourth laugh) that this really *is* the handout we'll be using, so they shouldn't crumple it up and throw it at you.

34

The "Great to be here" opening

THIS IS ONE OF THE OLDEST AND EASIEST OPENING lines to use.

You say:

"Thank you very much. It's great to be here in *(pull card out of your pocket and look at it)* Cleveland. *(Using name of city where you are)* "

That's it. A very simple sure-fire laugh. You can also use it as a callback (See Tip #50) by referring to the card a few times throughout the program. ("I must tell you that every time I'm speaking in ......Cleveland......I'm reminded of how wonderful the audiences are.")

Note: This joke only works if you're speaking in a city or town you don't live in. If you're speaking in the area where you live, it won't work.

35

The "I'm not being paid for this" opening

THIS IS AN OPENING THAT CAN WORK IN SEVERAL DIF-
ferent ways. The most common is if there is a t-shirt that is being
given out or sold to the audience as part of the event.

You say:

"Ladies & gentlemen, I want you to know I'm not being paid
for this presentation today. No, I'm receiving something *far* more
valuable than money. I'm receiving one of these (*hold up the t-shirt*).
It makes a wonderful souvenir of the event. Wash it once—and it
makes a nice little hand puppet. (*Hold your hand, as though the shirt
shrunk and is now a puppet.*) "

A few notes:

A. You are not limited to just using a t-shirt. You can use any
kind of shirt that the group has. And it doesn't have to be a
shirt they received at the event—it can be something they
have received before, or the business-casual golf shirt they

wear for work. But given a choice, a t-shirt is the funni-est item.

B. After you get the laugh on the "hand puppet" line, you can get a second laugh by saying, "No, this is a real collector's item. I'm going to sell mine on e-Bay tonight."

C. If there is no shirt to hold up, your strategy changes. A little research becomes necessary. You want to find out if there is someone in the group who most of the audience is aware of, who is very passionate about a sport or hobby. Then you say,
    "No, I'm receiving something *far* more valuable than money. I've been invited to go kayaking for a weekend with Ed Ericsson." (*Using whatever the hobby and person's name is*)

D. If you have several names to choose from, pick the one associated with the hobby that is the most unusual. "Invited to go to ten garage sales on a Saturday with Jim from accounting" is funnier than "Invited to go golfing with the CEO."

36

The "Could have listened to you all night" opening

THIS IS A GREAT OPENING IF THE SPEAKER BEFORE you is very long-winded.

You open by saying:

"Thank you, John. I must tell you, that was a wonderful speech you just gave. I could have listened to you talk all night. (*Pause*) And for a while there I thought I was going to *have* to."

A few notes:

A. This can also work if your introducer is long-winded. ("That was a wonderful introduction you gave me. ...")

B. The line works best if it refers to the speaker who immediately preceded you. However, you can refer to a speaker that was earlier in the day, or even earlier in the week (*if it's the same event*), and just change the way you posture the first sentence:

"I specifically enjoyed John Griffin's speech on Tuesday.

I could have listened to him talk all day. (*Pause*) And for a while there l thought I was going to *have* to."

C. It's better if the speaker you're poking fun of is present, but it's not absolutely necessary.

D. Make sure the speaker you're poking fun of isn't an icon or hero to this group, or you may alienate the audience. It's also a risky line to use if the speaker you're referring to is very elderly, or sick, or has something about them where the audience would feel badly that the speaker was long-winded. In that case, the audience probably wouldn't find it funny.

37

The "Personal attribute" opening

THIS IS WHERE YOU REFERENCE A PERSONAL ATTRI-
bute in order to get a laugh. These lines are usually self-deprecating,
so you must feel comfortable with your personal attribute you'll be
making fun of.

HAIR:

If you have a very unusual hair style, you could open with, "That is
the *last* time I use Super Cuts right before a speech."

If you are bald (and a man), you could have the last line in
your introduction be, "And former spokesman for the 'Hair Club
For Men'."

Or you could research someone else in your audience (known
to the group) who is also bald—and get their permission for you to
open with, "I've really been looking forward to being with all of you
today. As a matter of fact, I was telling that to Brian Smith (*use their
name*) just last week at our meeting of the 'Hair Club For Men.' (*It's*

imperative to get their permission, if you're going to share your self-deprecation with someone else!)

SIZE:

If you are particularly large, you can open with "I'm thrilled to be here. I just came from the all-you-can-eat buffet. I think the manager there is thrilled that I'm gone now."

If you're particularly short, you can open with, "Don't worry, I'll be short."

SPEECH:

If you speak with a thick accent, you can say, "I know what you're thinking. Great—another speaker from Alabama." (Pick a location where the accent sounds *nothing* like your accent—therein lies the humor!)

If you have a speech impediment, you could say, "If you think I'm hard to understand now, you should hear me when I'm drunk!"

NAME:

If you have a particularly long or complicated name, you can say, "Thank you for that nice introduction. You actually pronounced my name better than I can. Now let's see you try and spell it without looking at the notes."

As you can see, if you're going to be making fun of yourself, you must have a lot of confidence to pull it off. But references to your personal attributes are some of the easiest laughs to get, because you're being totally honest, and you're bringing up something that the entire audience is thinking about anyway.

38

The "Current event" opening

THIS IS AN OPENING THAT WORKS GREAT IF THERE'S something happening in the news that you can refer to. I'll give you two examples that worked well for me.

Several years ago I gave a speech for a company run by one of the owners of the Miami Heat, an NBA team. At the time of my speech, the NBA was on strike, with no end to the strike in sight.

I opened by saying, "I'm excited to be here, especially knowing that your president, Bob, is one of the owners of the Miami Heat. Now, I don't really follow basketball, so I don't know very much about the sport, but Bob was very nice. Instead of being paid for tonight, he gave me courtside tickets to all the Miami Heat games for the next two weeks. Well, I am so excited, I can't begin to tell you."

This got huge laughs, because it tied into a current event that everyone knew about, and it was "of the moment."

The other one that comes to mind was a speech I did for a company during the time that John Glenn had gone back into space, some thirty five years after his first historic flight.

I opened by saying, "I'm so excited to be here. I've been trying to get Steve (*the meeting planner*) to book me for this group for a long time. And I remember he told me years ago, 'David, the day they send John Glenn back into space is the day you'll get booked to speak to our group', and, well, here I am!"

Again, another big laugh, based on the current event. If you're going to use a current event reference, you need to pick an event that most everyone in the audience is aware of.

If the audience is all from the local area, you can use a local current event as your inspiration. I once did a program in northern California and read that morning's paper to look for ideas for an opening. There was a big feature story about a local shopping mall that used to be very popular, but had declined into somewhat of a "ghost" mall, with very few stores and very little traffic.

Based on that information, my opening was, "It's great to be here tonight. I was looking for a nice quiet place to rehearse this afternoon. Somewhere where I could be all alone. So I went to the Southside Mall." It got huge laughs from the audience, and I had never heard of that mall until reading their local paper.

If you pick a current event to reference, make sure that it is not something that is very controversial or sensitive, or the line may backfire—which is not the way to open a program!

39

The "Look around the room" opening

lots of opportunity

GOOD OBSERVATION CAN LEAD TO GREAT LAUGHS! You know from Tip #5 to always arrive early to check out the logistics of the room where you'll be speaking. There's another valuable reason to arrive early: There are often things about the room that lend themselves to humor that can be worked into your opening.

If the room is particularly sparse, you might open with, "I can see that most of your registration money (or "most of the capital improvement budget") went into decor."

If there are one or more large chandeliers, you might open with, "As you can see, we'll be doing our 'Phantom of the Opera' tribute, and you folks sitting under the chandeliers might want to rethink your seats."

If one wall is completely mirrored, you might open with, "Roxanne (*use name of meeting planner*) said, 'Wow, look at this turnout. We've got over 300 people!' and I said, 'Uh, no, Roxanne, those are mirrors over there. (*pointing to reflection of the audience in the mirrors*) We've only got about 150'."

If the wallpaper is gaudy, you might open with, "As I look at this wallpaper, I have to think there's a whole fleet of Dodge Neons driving around right now without seat covers."

You get the idea: Look around the room and see if there is something there that can be mined for humor. You can sometimes expand your horizon, and make reference to something funny about the hallway, the lobby, the bathroom, the parking lot—but it has to be something that almost everyone has also seen, or the line won't work.

40

The "Spontaneous" opening

BY ITS VERY NATURE, THIS IS NOT AN OPENING YOU can prepare. But it is an opening you can have your eyes open for. And most spontaneous openings, if they're funny, can get much bigger laughs than your best planned openings. The magic to spontaneity is that the audience realizes that what is happening is just for them, just for that very moment, never to be repeated again. That is why some speakers have a goal to always open with a spontaneous remark, and use their planned opening as a fallback.

Here's an example of a spontaneous opening that worked for me. I was the speaker at a luncheon. I followed the Pledge of Allegiance, which was led by the group's president. However, as the president led the group in the pledge, he turned toward the wall, but there was no flag. Everyone stood, recited the pledge, and sat down. I was then introduced.

I opened with, "It is my pleasure to be here this afternoon, especially having the distinct and esteemed honor of getting to follow the 'Pledge of Allegiance to the Wall of the United States of America'." Those who had already noticed there was no flag started

the big laugh, and were then joined by those who hadn't even realized there was no flag as they went through the rote recitation.

Tip #36 (The "Could have listened to you" opening) is basically a spontaneous opening, if used to reference the speaker immediately preceding you. More creative use of the spontaneous opening
comes with time and practice. And with time and practice comes
confidence that your zeroing in on something "of the moment" is
"on the money" for humor.

41

Acknowledge what's
going on around you

IF YOU ARE SPEAKING TO AN AUDIENCE, AND SOME-
thing out of the ordinary begins to occur (or has been happening
since you took the stage), you need to acknowledge it, albeit in a
humorous fashion. For example, if the microphone keeps going out,
you can say, "I'd like to thank Radio Shack for providing today's
equipment." (See Tip #63 for another use of "Radio Shack" in a
punch line.)

It's important for you to acknowledge when things go amiss,
because everyone in the room is seeing or hearing it just like you
are. If you ignore it, the crowd begins to get nervous, wondering if
the distraction is causing you stress. Or they may be wondering if
you're even aware of the occurrence in the room that everyone else
is experiencing.

Anything that happens that strays from the regular course of
events is worth mentioning. The vast majority of these things can
be referenced in a humorous way. (Microphone problems, computer

problems, lighting problems, noise from the next room, workmen coming in to fix the air conditioning, etc.)

Occasionally, there is an interruption that does *not* call for humor. (An audience member gets sick, a fire alarm goes off, someone comes in to announce a major news event, etc.) You must use common sense and refrain from using humor in those instances. But usually the things that happen around you are ripe fodder for laughs.

The key is for you to be willing to *say* what everyone else in the room is thinking at that moment. ("Is it just me, or is anyone else distracted by the folks outside our meeting room at the pool? I feel like I'm watching an episode of Baywatch in 3-D.")

Acknowledging what's going on around you leads directly into our next tip.

42

Spontaneity: "Speak now or forever hold your wit."

THE SHORTER THE TIME FROM THE "THINKING" OF something funny to the "saying" of something funny, the bigger the laugh. That is why it's important to say the funny thought as soon as possible after it hits you. Spontaneity, by its very definition, requires instant action.

You must still use good judgment on how you interject the line you've come up with. Normally, you're the one speaking, so your spontaneous line can come out of nowhere and (as long as it's funny) should get the anticipated laugh.

However, if you were participating on a panel, the spontaneous line might require interrupting someone else who is speaking—and that can be risky. You may come across as obnoxious, versus funny.

I have had success with one "interruption" line I use: Let's say another person on the panel is telling a story. If they have been talking for some time and they use the line, "And to make a long story short....," I quickly jump in with, "A little too late for that now."

Most of the time it gets a big laugh. Again, you must use your judgment. You probably wouldn't get a laugh from a crowd if you said that line to a long-winded member of the clergy. There's usually so much reverence for clergy and certain other professions, that the line would probably not work if it was targeted to them.

The key to this tip is to not let time lapse between your *thinking* of the line and then *saying* the line. It will do you no good to say, "Remember when the power went out two hours ago. Well, I'm wondering if we've paid the power bill recently" No, the line needs to be said *immediately* when the power goes out—"Hey, have you guys paid the power bill recently?" Not a hysterical line, but in the context of the moment it would get a laugh.

43

When in doubt, leave it out

THIS TIP IS THE COROLLARY TO TIP #42 (SPEAK NOW or forever hold your wit). When a funny line hits you spontaneously, and your mouth is preparing to utter the brilliance you've just come up with....sometimes another voice enters your head.

This is the voice of doubt, the voice of fear, the voice of reason, the voice that says, "Hey, maybe that line is a little bit over the top." Or offensive, or sensitive, or maybe just not funny. If you hear that voice creeping in, there's usually a reason. Your intuitive feelings and gut feelings on these kinds of things are usually tight.

So when in doubt, leave it out! As you become more proficient at getting laughs, you will fine-tune this hesitation, so that your judgment will become better and better at determining if the line is worth saying.

Sometimes your doubt is just coming from a lack of experience and a lack of confidence. The line may very well have gotten a good laugh. But allow yourself to build up that experience and confidence before starting to allow questionable lines to stay in.

Although this book will give you some good Silence Savers if a line doesn't work (Tip # 59), it's not a position you want to be in.

Sometimes you will only have a fraction of a second to decide whether a line is appropriate or not, and it's better to err on the side of caution and leave it out.

You will also have many times when you are writing material that will be used in the future, when you're not pressured with the instant decision of whether to use certain lines or not. However, you will still have to decide if the lines are appropriate or not. And, again, it can't be made any simpler: When in doubt, leave it out!

44

Brevity is the soul of wit

THIS GEM COMES FROM A MR. WILLIAM SHAKESPEARE, who was pretty adept at getting audiences laughing. (Well, except when he was presenting his tragedies). What it means is: The less words you can use to get your laugh, the better.

In most cases, words will be the tools you'll use to get your laugh. The more quickly and more simply you can express your humorous thought, the stronger that laugh will be.

You may remember from Tip #17 (If you must tell a joke....) that the longer a joke is, the funnier the punchline had better be. With every added word you use, there is an additional investment in time and energy from the listener. And that investment demands a big payoff, or there is disappointment.

Often some of your biggest laughs can come from very few words. Sometimes one carefully selected word is all it takes to send a crowd into regales of laughter. And that one word can be used as a callback (See Tip # 50) to get laughs throughout your program.

When you are writing humor, go back and keep editing. Keep removing all the unnecessary words. Find a simpler way to say it. Find a shorter way to say it. When you remove the fat, the steak is much, much tastier.

If your laughs are being derived from something other than words, (props, magic, juggling, etc.), the same rule applies. There's nothing more frustrating than watching a ten-minute magic trick that culminates in a lackluster punchline.

However, you can create a very entertaining ten-minute magic trick or a fifteen-minute story or any other "longer" segment of your presentation by adding laugh lines continually along the way.

If you keep the audience entertained throughout the "journey" with laugh "spikes" along the way, you then have permission to tell a long story. If the laughs in your story were to be charted on paper, it should look like a (healthy!) EKG. That's why I call them laugh "spikes," because they keep coming in regular intervals and continue to "spike" the interest of the audience.

But if you see them starting to look at their watches or their phones, you're probably using too many words! Keep it short!

45

Write it down now—or forget it

AS YOU CONTINUE TO CREATE HUMOR FOR YOUR presentations, you will find yourself developing your skill to "think more funny."

You will develop a keen sense of observation and a "comic view" for everything around you.

You will find humor in places where you never thought there could be anything funny.

You will think of funny things at times and in places when you least expect it.

And all of it will be for naught *if you don't write it down when you think of it!*

I say "write it down" as an old-school generic phrase. More than likely you will be putting your ideas in your phone or your computer—anything that gives you the ability to capture your creativity immediately.

We human beings fool ourselves into thinking that the brilliant thought we came up with is so funny and so clever, there's no possible way that we could forget it. This couldn't be farther from the truth.

When your funny ideas are created "out of context" (for example, in the shower), that lack of context becomes the disconnect for why you can't remember a few hours later "that hysterical thing I thought of this morning in the shower."

It's important to have a tool for capturing your ideas with you at all times in order to start building your humor strength. (A large percentage of your best laugh ideas will come while driving, so make sure you have a hands-free way of recording your thoughts!)

So don't fall into the easy trap of being *so* impressed with your funny thought that you're *certain* you'll remember it later. It's likely that you won't.

If you're serious about adding humor to your presentations, keep the tools with you at all times to capture the funny ideas that come to you when you're nowhere near an audience.

46

The Rule of Three

THIS IS ONE OF THOSE TECHNIQUES THAT COMEDI-
ans have been using for centuries. I'm sure that even the funnier
cavemen were etching three drawings on the wall of their caves—
the first two normal, the third one funny.

That is the essence of the Rule of Three—a list of three
things; with the first two being perceived as "normal" or fitting to
the idea being conveyed, and the third one catching the listener by
surprise in its outlandish contrast to the others.

Notice I said "listener." The Rule of Three is designed to be
enjoyed by the ear. While it can work in print, it doesn't have the
same impact that hearing it can. There is a rhythm that is created
with the three items, regardless of how short or long each item is.
(Although shorter is always better—See Tip # 44.)

Here's an example from one of my programs: "I remember
when I first started in this business years ago. I had dreams. I had
hopes. I had....hair."

With the setup, the listener is expecting to hear something like "I had dreams. I had hopes. I had courage." Instead, they're hearing "I had dreams. I had hopes. I had....hair." (I take an ever-so-slight pause before the word "hair. ") They're surprised and they laugh.

Another example: "One day we're hoping to open offices in several major cities. New York. Los Angeles. Okeechobee."

And it can be in the form of longer sentences or a series of questions: "How many of you have ever run a marathon? "How many of you have ever run a half-marathon?" "How many of you haven't gotten off your couch since the late 1990's?"

If you need to list more than two "normal" items in order to make a point in your presentation, don't make your fourth one or fifth one a funny one. You still may get a laugh, but it won't have the power that the Rule of Three gives you.

You can also do multiple Rules of Three in a row, which begins to build anticipation with the audience with each successive one.

47

Brand names are funnier than generic names

"DODGE DART" IS FUNNIER THAN "COMPACT CAR."

"Skippy" is funnier than "peanut butter."

"Captain Crunch" is funnier than "cereal."

"Lazy Boy" is funnier than "recliner."

"Ikea" is funnier than "furniture store."

"Home Depot" is funnier than "hardware store."

Any questions?

When you have the opportunity, use a brand name of a product or service, rather than just saying the generic name. "So there we were, sitting at the Dairy Queen, in our formal wear" is funnier than "So there we were, sitting at the ice cream shop, in our formal wear."

This isn't rocket science—it's just that brand names sound funnier!

48

Odd numbers are funnier than even numbers

I'VE BEEN GETTING LAUGHS FROM AUDIENCES FOR over thirty years and why this one works is still a mystery to me.

Given the same line, you will get a bigger laugh by saying "We drove around for eleven hours before I would ask for directions" than with "We drove around for ten hours before I would ask for directions." Or twelve hours. It doesn't matter—the odd numbers work better. Trust me, I've tried it both ways.

This is one of those "unsolved mysteries" of comedy. But my best guess is that odd numbers just feel funnier than even ones.

49

"Oops, I did it again"
—Use planned mistakes

THE FIRST TIME I SAW A "PLANNED MISTAKE" DONE IN a live setting was many years ago while watching comedian Steve Martin in concert.

If memory serves me, about midway through the show, he said, "I'm now going to do a very beautiful love song. If we could have the blue lighting now, please." He sat there for about five seconds, waiting for the blue lighting, which never appeared. He appeared to get irritated and then tried to save face by saying, "No, actually, the white lighting is much better. Thank you. We'll leave it this way."

This was a classic illustration of a planned mistake. He, of course, asked for the blue lighting at *every* show, and it would never appear. Steve Martin did not originate this bit, as it has been around since vaudeville. "Planned mistakes" have been getting laughs since comedians have been getting laughs.

Here's an example of one I have used. You put a word that is hard to pronounce into your presentation. When you get to that word, you stumble on it. You then try to pronounce it a second time and stumble on it again. The third time you use a synonym or phrase that means the same thing as the word you're having difficulty saying. It looks like this:

"There's a colloquialism. *(stumble on the pronunciation)* Uh, a colloquialism. *(stumble again)* You know, there's an old saying....."

This particular planned mistake works well if your program includes very technical or multi-syllabic words that are specific to your industry. The audience can relate to the difficulty of pronouncing some of those words they deal with on a day-to-day basis.

Planned mistakes can run the gamut from subtle to slapstick. One speaker might elect to run to the stage and "accidentally" trip and fall on the floor, causing gasps and surprise from the audience. At which point, the speaker looks up and says, "I will now take questions from the floor." He gets his laugh, he gets up, and begins his program.

Just like Steve Martin's "blue lighting" example, planned mistakes can involve other audiovisual equipment. You can have an LCD projector begin to "not work" and be forced to start doing hand shadows on the wall. You can "try" to get your PowerPoint program running and accidentally put up "the wrong slide deck" or some document that nobody should see.

One word of caution: If you are speaking to the same audience more than once, you can't use the same planned mistake more than once! It typically won't get a laugh a second time, once they realize the whole thing is a sham. But it's not that difficult to come up with new planned mistakes that will generate laughs.

The reason these planned mistakes work so well is that audiences love to see vulnerability on the part of a speaker. It makes the speaker much more human. The audience sees the speaker up there having to deal with the mistake and it causes them to laugh (all the while thinking to themselves, "I'm glad I'm not up there!").

Many of the best "planned mistakes" come from real mistakes that happened to a speaker that generated huge laughs. The speaker then finds a way to replicate the same thing that happened every time he or she speaks!

50

Use callbacks

CALLBACKS ARE ONE OF THE MOST CLASSIC TECH-
niques used in getting laughs. Here's how it works.

Let's say you used Tip #31 (The "We're here for three hours"
opening) where you stomp your foot three times. As you move
through the program you would "call back" to that earlier laugh by
once again stomping your foot three times.

You wouldn't need any kind of setup, as the audience already
knows what's funny about it from before. Just the mere mention of
something "stupid" would warrant the foot stomping....and generate
the laugh.

You can sometimes do a callback of an earlier laugh as many
as five or six times in one program. However, you start to come up
against the law of diminishing returns if you use the same callback
more than six times.

You are not limited to referencing just one laugh line for your
callbacks. You can have multiple callbacks going on throughout the
program. I've seen some speakers do a closing that incorporated

callbacks from almost two-dozen laugh lines they had used throughout the program. (A very well-crafted and very powerful closing!)

A word of caution: Don't put in a callback just for the sake of using one. It must have a *reason* to be there and relate to the point being made in the speech at that moment. The humor is derived from the current point in the speech being tied in (cleverly) to the item from earlier.

51

Try a new laugh line at least three times

I THINK IT WAS LIONEL RICHIE WHO WROTE, "YOU'RE once, twice, three times a laugh line." Then he changed "laugh line" to "lady" and had a huge hit!

OK, that's not true. But that "original" lyric could definitely have been geared to readers like you who might get frustrated after a first attempt at trying a new funny line or bit.

If you come up with something you think should get a laugh—anything from a one-liner to a prop to a funny PowerPoint slide—and it doesn't get the laugh you envisioned, *don't* base your decision whether to use it again on the reaction of that first audience.

Unless you get a violent negative reaction, booing and hissing and objects being thrown at you, you owe it to yourself to try it again.

As it is, a real negative reaction to an attempt at humor is extremely rare. Odds are more likely that your hesitation to do the piece of material again will come from a lukewarm response from the audience—or even worse, silence. You'd almost *rather* get booing than silence.

If a line doesn't work the first time out, you've *got* to try it again. Sometimes it's just your nervousness of trying a new line that gives it a less-than-stellar delivery the first time out—and the second time is a charm.

Any lack of confidence or hesitation on your delivery diminishes the potential that the line will work. And we tend to have some hesitation, however subtle, on a new line that doesn't offer the same comfort level as something we've used time and time again.

If the material doesn't work the second time, you probably feel as though you have definitely proven that line is not going to work. Well, painful as it might be, you've got to try it *one more time* before dropping it. You might have just caught two bad audiences in a row—-or you might have delivered the line with hesitation two times in a row.

You owe it to yourself to try it a third time before filing the line away. (Never throw out material that doesn't work—file it. Create a humor file called "Lines That Should Have Worked." You may be able to go back to it someday and re-work it, re-write it, or even re-use it, as is, in a better fit.)

52

Hire a professional humor writer (AKA: The Shameless Plug!)

THE READER MIGHT THINK THIS TIP IS NOTHING more than a shameless plug for the work I do for leaders, managers, salespeople, trainers, writers, etc. And while that may be true, there actually is an important point to be made here.

If you truly want to get big laughs from any audience, sometimes it pays to have a professional help you through the process. If you were to utilize every tip in this book, you'd have a robust and varied arsenal of funny material that could keep your audiences laughing for decades. But sometimes you may need a little help to take the ideas and actually develop them to work specifically for *you*.

When clients hire me for humor writing, it's usually for something known as "humor punchups." This is a process where the clients give me their existing speech or slides or curriculum or book, and I "punch it up" by adding laugh lines throughout. These lines do not detract from the message at hand, but, rather, add laugh "spikes" (See Tip #44) along the way, like blips on an EKG.

I often hire attorneys, accountants, graphic designers, publicists, and other professionals for things that I *can* do, but not always well. Or I hire them because it takes me ten hours of my time to do the project, versus, perhaps, one hour of their time. Just because you *can* do something, doesn't mean you *should* do something, especially if someone else can do it better or far more efficiently.

This is one of the key tenets of time management. Don't waste your time on tasks that bog you down—get others to do them and free yourself up to concentrate on the things that you do best and where you provide the most value.

If creating humor is something that you love to do, but is not something that comes easy to you, it is really in your best interest to hire someone to help you. It doesn't matter *how* you make your presentation funnier—as long as you do.

And while I'd love to be able to personally help you with your "humor punchups," you're certainly not limited to my (really incredible) help, which you can learn about at www.FunnierSpeeches.com or by e-mailing David@DavidGlickman.com.

Seriously, there are plenty of other humor writers, comedy coaches, and professionals out there who can be of service to you. A search of the Internet under "comedy writers" or "humor writers" will give you many, many choices.

At the time this book is being written there's a relatively new business called www.ComedyWire.com that also offers humor punchups and appears to be a very good service. And while I personally can't vouch for the quality of their punchups, at least I can give you a first step in checking out other options besides me.

One note: Once you have chosen a humor writer, you should probably begin with a small project. This helps you make sure you're happy with what the writer can create for you, before investing a lot of your money.

53

Do try this at home—
You *can't* practice too much

MAKE SURE YOU READ THIS TITLE THE RIGHT WAY. Don't misunderstand it to mean that if you practice too much it will start to work against you. No, no, no, it's exactly the opposite: You can't practice too much.

Meaning that the more you practice your laugh lines, the better you will do. There is no such thing as practicing too much—you *can't* practice too much!

In order for humor to work, it must appear effortless. It must appear smooth. Any tip you decide to try from the book should be rehearsed as much as possible before actually saying or doing it in front of an audience. The only ones you can't practice are the spontaneous lines. But everything you have planned for the purposes of getting a laugh should be practiced.

How do you practice?

Out loud.

Standing up. (Or sitting down, if that's the way you'll be doing your presentation.)

You want to replicate the same feelings you'll have and the same movements you'll have to make. If you'll be using a hand-held microphone, use a hairbrush or something to simulate the mike in your hand. It is not necessary to rehearse in front of a mirror, unless you're doing something that's very visual and you want to see how it looks. Otherwise, practicing in front of a mirror can often be more distracting than helpful.

As you become more and more comfortable at getting laughs from your audiences, you'll probably be tempted to cut back on your rehearsal. Try to avoid this temptation. Even the pros continue to rehearse, especially as they add new material to their presentations.

Any nervousness you feel when presenting should be geared to the question of whether the material is going to work and *not* to the question of whether you're sufficiently prepared. The former you have little control over, and your nervousness is acceptable. The latter you have every bit of control over, and you should work towards giving the most professional presentation possible.

Have I mentioned that you can't practice too much?

54

Humor on the screen

MANY, IF NOT MOST, PRESENTATIONS TODAY USE
some kind of visuals on a screen to supplement what the speaker is
saying. The key word in that sentence is "supplement."

When it comes to adding humor to a presentation, I am a firm
believer that your slides or videos can certainly serve as one more
way to get laughs from your audience—but that you shouldn't rely
on your screen humor to be your *only* source of humor.

The reason is this: Technology Is Risky. Every person reading this book has been in the audience of a presenter who has had
their technology go awry during a presentation. Or perhaps *you* were
the presenter—and suffered through the frustration (and panic) of
having to present your program without all the technology you had
planned for.

So with the caveat in place that any humor on the screen will
be supplemental *only*—and that you will be prepared to get lots of
laughs from the many *other* techniques in this book—let's talk about
ways to get laughs from the screen.

Your slides can simply be a funny cartoon or a funny photo that illustrates your point. The internet is your oyster when it comes to finding funny visuals. Two things to keep in mind:

1. If you're finding it on the internet, there's a good chance some of your audience members have seen it, too—which definitely dilutes the impact of the humor That's why original humor is usually better.

2. You need to make sure that you're legally permitted to show the images you're showing.

Many presenters ignore the legalities of what they can and cannot show—and just take the attitude of "Well, I found it on the internet, so I'm going to show it." I am not an attorney, so I am not in a position to give legal advice on this issue. But, suffice to say, most images that you find on-line are owned by *somebody*—and there is often a royalty to be paid or a license to be purchased to show the image.

The same thing applies to funny videos you may want to show. Just because a video is posted on YouTube doesn't mean you can legally show it. You don't always know if whomever posted it did so legally. But, again, I'm not in a position to be giving legal advice here. For the purposes of our discussion, we will assume you have permission to show any funny photos or videos you choose to use.

If you are going to use a funny video, you should keep it as short as possible to make your point as quickly as possible. Or perhaps just show an excerpt of it. Audience members are used to "clicking away" from a video they are getting bored with—but don't have that luxury as an audience member. Help them out and keep your videos short. I always say, "Get the laugh and get out."

I think it's better to use original humor on the screen. Perhaps you could have a bullet point that reads, "I put this one here just to see if anyone is even reading these slides."

Or have the slides get into an argument with you—where the slides take on a mind of their own.

Or maybe you switch quickly to the next slide—and have that copy say, "Wait! Wait! We didn't get to write everything down from the last slide!"

In other words, you break down the "wall" between the speaker and the screen and have the slides become another "presenter" in the program. You have a "conversation" *with your slides.*

In Tip #67 (Customized parody book covers) we will discuss one idea for humor on the screen that warrants its own chapter. Frankly, I could probably write an entire book just on ideas for Screen Humor. Original videos, animation, audience polling, social media feeds......there are a myriad of additional ways that presenters are using the screen to generate laughs.

But for the purposes of *this* book, it's important that you learn how to add humor to any presentation without having to rely on any technology. Then if you *do* decide to use the screen for humor, it becomes a great addition to the program, but not your only lifeline for laughs.

55

Poke fun at the competition

MANY BUSINESS BOOKS CAUTION YOU NOT TO TALK negatively about your competitors. However, if you can posture that "negative" comment into a "funny" comment, you can usually get in a light "jab" at the competition with little or no fallout.

For example: "It's a pleasure to be meeting here today at the Hilton. We like to meet in a place that fits our image. There are several places in the area available for meetings. For example, (*Name of competitor*) usually has their meetings at the Motel 6."

You could also use Tip #31 and make the punchline about the competitor. "We're here for three hours….or if we have anyone here from (*Name of competitor*) that's (*stomp foot three times*).

Now, of course, the audience knows that you *wouldn't* have someone from the competition in the room, but they suspend their disbelief and laugh anyway.

There's also the possibility for spontaneous humor. If you're speaking and the audience hears a loud bang or plates dropping in another (or your) meeting room, you could say, "Oh, it sounds like the (*Name of competitor*) shipping department."

Because these kind of lines are designed to get laughs in a relatively harmless manner, you remove the stigma associated with "making fun of the competition" and yet are doing just that!

How do you know if you've crossed the line in making fun of the competition? The audience will tell you. Instead of—or in addition to—a laugh, you will hear a very loud and audible "Ooh!"

"Ooh!" means the audience thinks you may have gone too far. In that case, you try a saver line ("Oh, I see we've moved from the humor portion to the drama portion. My mistake") and then make a note not to use the offending line again.

56

Don't condone "politically incorrect" remarks

HOPEFULLY, YOU HAVE EMBRACED THE WISDOM IN keeping all of your remarks "politically correct" when speaking in public. That means avoiding attempts at humor that involve racial, ethnic, religious, and sexist themes. (Also remember Tip #20—Avoid political humor)

There are *plenty* of other ways for you to get laughs without stepping into this dangerous territory. Subjects that are freely joked about in comedy clubs and television sitcoms are not acceptable in a business or public setting.

Now, that being said, in order to present yourself in the best possible light, you need to take it one step further. Your refraining from these remarks is not enough. If someone in your *audience* makes a politically incorrect remark or asks a politically incorrect question—especially one that gets a laugh—you cannot condone the remark.

You cannot ignore the fact that it's been said, or join in the laughter (difficult as that sometimes can be). The good news is that If the remark is really off base, there will be *no* laughter, and your job becomes a little easier.

The beauty of this tip is that you can *still* get a laugh while making your point that you don't buy into the remark that's been made.

Your reply can be something like: "Well, I can see who won't be nominated for the Nobel Peace Prize this year."

Or: "I'm guessing you're not active with the Anti-Defamation League."

Or: "You *do* realize you're not on Twitter right now using an anonymous name?"

Basically, you throw a mild insult at the offender and then move on. You do not want to belabor the remark any further, or you risk the tone changing from "light" to "fight."

Even after you have made it clear that you won't tolerate politically incorrect humor, you may still have a second or third audience member give it a try. You can make your point again simply by saying, "Have you met this guy over here?," referring to the person who made the initial remark. You may also be able to use some of the heckler comebacks listed in the next two tips.

57

"Safe" heckler comebacks

EVERY TIME YOU STEP UP TO A MICROPHONE, YOU risk having someone in the audience yell something at you. This is not always a bad thing. Sometimes someone will say something that is very funny and doesn't harm your program. It actually adds to it.

In those cases, you are best served by laughing along, perhaps asking that person to stand for applause, pretending to write down what was said so that you could use it again.

But this tip is geared for those other times when the remark may not be so positive. Hecklers are typically not prevalent in business settings like they would be in a comedy club. However, there are still folks out there whose goal is to derail you with a remark or a laugh at your expense.

Your first response to a heckler should be light. The heckler usually just wants attention. Sometimes you can find a way to involve them in your program so that they get the attention they're desiring (or craving).

But if you'd rather just throw out a line to deal with the interruption, here are a few "mild" ones that have worked well for me:

"Sorry, but I work alone."

"Gee, I'm sorry we don't have microphones for all of you."

"*(Directly into the mike)* Security, table 7. Security, table 7."

"When you go the movies, do you talk back to the screen?"

"Is the bar open this early?" or "I remember when I had *my* first beer."

"Listen, I've only got 20 minutes to make a fool of myself, you've got all night."

Don't be a surprised if a heckler comes up to you after a program and says, "Boy, I really helped you, didn't I?"

Most of them sincerely believe that a funny presenter *wants* to be heckled so that the funny presenter can rebound with a funny comeback line. And if you're doing your job right, you're being perceived as a "funny presenter" and may be subjected to some of the risks associated with that accomplishment.

58

"Risky" heckler comebacks

RARELY HAVE I USED THESE LINES IN A BUSINESS SET-
ting, but I thought I'd share them with you. If your heckler is relent-
less, and your first or second "safe" comeback didn't work, here are
a few rougher (risky) ones:

"I'm guessing the tractor pull was canceled tonight."

"It's so sad when cousins marry."

"Look, I have a mike, God has a plan, and you're not in it.
Any questions?"

"Do you work at being annoying, or does it come easy to you?"

Again, the odds of having to use one of these lines with an
audience outside of a comedy club are very slim. However, if your
heckler just keeps going, you can try to change the momentum by
saying, "How many of you would like to see this gentleman stop
interrupting and let us continue the program?" (This is the "G"
rated version of the question. It's worded somewhat differently in
comedy clubs.)

You'll usually get a loud cheer, and it often will finally put the heckler in his place. (If you don't get a loud cheer, you may be in for a rough program!)

If the situation is intolerable, you might just say, "Ladies and gentlemen, as you can see, we have a challenge here. I have worked very hard on preparing today's program for you, but you cannot get the most out of it under these conditions. So here's what we're going to do. We're going to take a short break, about five minutes, to take care of the problem. So, I'll see you in a few minutes."

Then it is up to the powers that be to remove the "problem." If *you* are the "powers that be," then you may have to call security (or the police) to remove the person.

Sometimes you can simply talk to the heckler during this unplanned break and make a polite but firm request that they refrain from any more interruptions.

But if it's reached the point where you've had to actually stop the program, chances are the person's behavior has reached the level where you and your audience are best served by the person's removal.

59

Silence Savers

WHOEVER SAID "SILENCE IS GOLDEN" HAS NEVER tried to make a group of people laugh!

"Silence is deadly" if you've just said a line that was *supposed* to get a laugh and it didn't! But never fear, Silence Savers are here!

Silence Savers are typically self-deprecating lines that get a laugh based on your poking fun of the situation you're in. The best example of someone who used Silence Savers to extricate himself from material that wasn't working was the late *Tonight Show* host, Johnny Carson.

Many viewers thought he deliberately would drop in some "clunkers" into his nightly monologue, so that he could use a Silence Saver. (While he did put a few deliberate ones in sketches like "Carnac"—designed to set up a funny insult aimed at his announcer, Ed McMahon, or at the audience—he *never* deliberately put a bad joke into a monologue.)

Here are a few Silence Savers that always seem to work:

"This is good. I was looking for a nice quiet place to rehearse tonight."

"Wow, when you guys get quiet, you don't fool around."

"That's ok. I can wait."

"Have l said something to upset you people?"

"And right about now, *(name of person in charge)* is thinking, 'Whose idea was it to have *(your last name)* get up here and speak?'"

"You know, that one was hysterical on paper."

"*(to a lone laugher)* If you could just run around the room and sound like a crowd, this will go a lot easier for me."

"Wow, and I thought that one would *kill*."

You should only use one Silence Saver at a time—one after each line that gets silence. After you get your laugh from the Silence Saver, then you move back into your program and your next line.

The Silence Savers are most effective if they are scattered throughout the program. (Well, actually, they are most effective if you don't have to use them at all! Using them means something didn't work.)

If you hit a spot in the program where several lines in a row aren't working, and each one is followed in succession by a Silence Saver, you can get laughs from about three in a row before you start to feel the effects of the law of diminishing returns.

After that point, the audience may start to get uncomfortable. You can also use a callback at that point, even as a non-sequitur, to try to get the crowd back again.

Fortunately, if you diligently follow the tips in this book, you will rarely be faced with the threat of having to use more than three Silence Savers in a row. But, as you know from Tip #10, on any given day your audience may be difficult and these Silence Savers may be a real lifeline.

60

The "Audience is in on the joke" bit

THIS IS A GREAT BIT TO USE IF YOU WILL BE ADDRESS-
ing a smaller audience first, who are also part of a bigger audience
you will be speaking to later.

This typically might happen if you are conducting a leadership meeting and then speaking at a session of all employees.

Or if you are delivering a breakout session at a meeting and
then are doing a general session later. Here's how the bit works:

When you are speaking to the smaller audience first, do Tip
#28 (The "Car in the parking lot" opening). After you get your
laugh, tell them that you want them to be part of a joke you are
going to do at the later session.

Explain that you are going to be doing the *same* joke again
at the session with the bigger audience. When you say the punchline that ends with the phrase "....so if you could move it (*the green
1997 Dodge Neon*), they'd appreciate it," everyone from the smaller

audience should get up—*in unison*—and start to head for the door, as though it's their car.

The more the smaller audience (with whom you're setting it up) is spread out throughout the larger audience later, the funnier the joke is visually. But it will still work even if the smaller audience is all at a head table—and all get up in unison to move the offending green Neon. Once the bigger audience laughs—and they will—you can simply say, "OK, you can all go back to your seats now. Let's give a nice hand to the (*name of organization*) comedy troupe. They handled that like real pros!"

61

The "That's French for......" bit

THIS BIT WORKS GREAT IF YOU ARE SPEAKING SOME-where that has a very foreign-sounding name. It can be the name of the town, the name of the county, the name of the building, the name of the meeting room you're in, etc. And it doesn't have to be French—I just picked that one for the title.

For example, you would say, "It's great to be here at the Anatole Hotel. 'Anatole' is a French word that means 'vastly overpriced'."

You select the language that sounds closest to the foreign-sounding name you're going to poke fun at. You say: "it's a (*name of language*) word that means" and then pick the most obvious thing that people are thinking about that town or room, etc. Your laugh is coming from the fact that you're saying what everybody is thinking.

Here are a few different examples of how it can be used:

"It's great to be here in beautiful Las Palmas. 'Las Palmas' is a Spanish term that means 'overpriced real estate'."

(Notice I said Spanish "term," not Spanish "word." That's because "Las Palmas" is more than one word, therefore "term" would be more appropriate. If the name of the place is even longer you can say "phrase" instead of word. Or you can simply say, "Las Palmas is Spanish for... ')

"It's great to be here in the Mohave-Apache Room. 'Mohave-Apache' is an old Native American term that means 'very ugly wallpaper'."

"It's great to be here in Duluth. 'Duluth' is Scandinavian for 'nothing to do in town at night'."

"I hope you enjoyed the meal. That was "Linguine Alfredo" which is Italian for "we went cheap on the dinner budget."

If you're not sure of the derivation of the word you're poking fun at, you can be generic and say, "It's an old European word that means..." or "It's an old Latin American word that means..." You can even make it totally generic by saying, "It's a foreign word that means. . .." but that's not as funny as being more specific to what language the word is derived from.

Please note that you're *not* making fun of the language—or the people who speak that language—when you do this bit. You are making fun of something about the location. You are simply using the foreign-sounding word as the vehicle to poke fun at something *else*.

If you do the bit properly, no one will associate the joke you're making with the nationality of the people whose language you're referring to. The humor lies totally in the target you're making fun of, which is probably on everyone's mind anyway.

62

The "Here's what you missed" bit

THIS IS A BIT YOU CAN USE WHEN YOU HAVE BEGUN your program and a latecomer enters the room. As the latecomer takes their seat, you break from your program as quickly as you comfortably can, and acknowledge their entrance: "Hi there. Welcome. Don't worry, you haven't missed much."

That is your cue to then go through a rapid-fire summary of "what they missed" before they came in. This bit will only work if the person is at least three minutes late, so that you have enough material you've already said that you can then "sum up" quickly.

The bit will work even better if the latecomer arrives near the end of your program. In that case, your summary hits more of the highlights of the program, versus the quick summation of everything you've said if the person is only a few minutes late. When it comes to this bit, "the later, the greater!"

The key to this bit's success is the lightning fast delivery of "what they missed." You are not doing it word-for-word, but, rather, you are paraphrasing what you already said.

Because it is hard to speak at that pace and remain understandable, you will probably want to have this bit very well-rehearsed before you attempt it. Feel free to use your notes to help keep you on track. However, if this is a program you do often, you will probably reach a point where you can recite this quick summary from memory.

If you like this bit, the good news is that you will typically have at least one latecomer to any program. I've gone as far as pre-arranging someone to come in late, because the bit works so well.

63

The "Fake mike failure" bit

WHEN YOU CHECK OUT YOUR MICROPHONE BEFORE
the program (Tip #5), see if it's the kind that has an On-Off switch
on the side. if it does, you can get a good laugh from this bit.

You can do this bit anywhere in the program, but I'd advise
you to do it at least five minutes into the program, once you're getting laughs and have established your "humor credibility."

Start speaking about something that is not crucial that your
audience hear. As you are talking, subtly take your finger and switch
"off" the microphone. You will need to rehearse this, so that it will
not appear as though you are turning it off.

You should be able to do this with one finger on the same
hand that is holding the microphone. If you need to use your other
hand, the bit starts to lose its effectiveness, because it's obvious you're
turning the mike off. (If the mike has its On-Off switch on the bottom of the mike, it is very difficult to make this work. It really needs
to be on the side for this bit to work smoothly.)

As you switch off the mike, keep talking for five seconds, so that the audience (and you) have come to the realization that the microphone has "failed."

You then fiddle with the mike, like you're trying to fix it. Perhaps shake it around. in doing so, you subtly switch the mike back "on", so that it's working. Now here comes the laugh.

Once you've got it working again, you say, "Oh, I guess we must have borrowed this mike from....." and you say the name of a competing organization. It's just a gentle poke—and an easy laugh—at the expense of a competing business.

If you're running an association meeting, you can say the name of another group that you compete with for members.

Or you could say, "We must have borrowed this mike from the folks who are repairing the Main Street overpass," or some local project that is going slowly or not doing well. Even though the folks repairing the Main Street overpass wouldn't *have* a microphone, the audience still laughs because you're comparing the mike's effectiveness to the effectiveness of the entity you're making fun of.

If you just want to keep the joke generic, you can simply say, "I'd like to thank Radio Shack for supplying today's equipment." (Even though a Radio Shack microphone is probably more reliable than a hotel mike, it still gets a laugh because the Radio Shack brand is not perceived to be high-end equipment.)

You can also use this bit if your microphone actually *does* stop working, but you get a much bigger laugh when you're in control of the situation and the mike is only "out" for a few seconds.

64

The "Cell phone" bit

NO MATTER HOW MANY TIMES, HOW NICELY, OR HOW emphatically the audience is asked to turn off their cell phones before a program or a meeting, there will inevitably be at least one or two phones that still ring during your remarks. This bit will help you get some laughs when it happens.

Place your cell phone in your pocket, or on a table or lectern near you, so that it is easily within your reach. When you hear the cell phone in the audience ring, stop your remarks, reach for *your* cell phone, and pretend that it is *yours* that is ringing. The audience will know that it is not your phone, and can usually even pinpoint by the sound of the ring, where (or in a small crowd, who) it is coming from.

Fiddle with your phone as though you're trying to answer it, and as soon as the ringing in the audience stops, you say into your phone (and into the microphone):

"Hello. (*long pause*) Nothing. (*as though you were asked, "What are you doing?"*)

Oh, I'm just running a meeting (*or giving a speech, etc.*)

Oh, no, it's fine. They don't care. Everyone's got their phones out. Nobody cares. Half the room is checking e-mail.

They think I don't see them. Someone's checking voice-mail. I might as well be doing shadow puppets up here. Well, look, l probably should get back to the meeting here. Take care, and call me back anytime. lt's ok. Nobody cares. Bye."

While it may not stop the cell phones from ringing, the bit does get a good laugh. It also directly addresses the frustration that many in the audience feel when they hear a cell phone ring during a program. When you do the "cell phone bit," make sure your voice sounds very cheery and upbeat. You cannot sound angry, or the moment can become awkward.

Also, the "cell phone bit" will only work once in a program. If a phone rings again, you can get maybe one more laugh out of it by doing a callback and reaching for your phone a second lime. But beyond that, you need to ignore the ringing phone(s) and keep going with your program.

65

The more *specific* the humor, the more *terrific* the humor

WHEN YOU ARE CREATING HUMOR FOR YOUR PRO-
grams, you generally have a very specific audience in mind. They
may be your follow employees, professional colleagues, prospects
for your product, members of your civic organization, and so on.
You should try to tailor as much of your humor specifically to
that audience—make it about them or something that only they
would understand.

The good news is that the laughs generated by specific humor
are typically far greater than the laughs generated by generic humor.
Because it is considered "inside" information—and the audience
has a sense that they are in on a "private joke" just for them—they
respond much more favorably.

The equally good news is that specific humor is actually easier
to write than generic humor. It is much easier to zero in on specific
foibles, hot buttons, or personalities of a group, than it is to create
humor that will work for any audience, regardless of their purpose
in gathering.

And while this book is designed to help you get any audience laughing—you will have an easier time doing so if you can customize your humor to the group.

Some of the next few tips address some great ways to customize the humor specifically to a given audience. However, to be able to create the specific humor, you must do a little research about your audience and the event where you'll be speaking. The next tip shows you how to do that.

66

Get the scoop on the group

THE FOLLOWING IS THE QUESTIONNAIRE I USE before speaking to any group. Because I do this for a living, the list of questions is quite extensive—and is probably *way* more information than you would want before your presentation.

However, the better you know your group going in, the better you can craft your customized humor. Also, the better you know your group going in, the easier it is to ad-lib a funny remark during your talk.

The questionnaire I use is divided into two parts. Part 1 is questions about the event itself. This information will help you visualize exactly what the scenario will be like. The more you can visualize the logistics of the program beforehand, the more successful you will be.

Part 2 is questions about the group. Again, you can gather as much or as little information as you want but when it comes to humor, knowledge is power. Frankly, you can't know too much about your audience.

Most of the time I do the research on the phone and the group never even sees the questions. The questionnaire is really more for my benefit, to help guide the phone call. And I find I get much better information if I talk to them directly, versus having them filling out the forms.

Also, the vast majority of my presentations are for work-related audiences. Many of these questions are not applicable if you are presenting at a social event or one that has nothing to do with the attendees' jobs.

PART 1 — QUESTIONS ABOUT THE EVENT

1. Dates for entire event (please send full agenda, if possible)

2. Timeline for my program (other presentations, what's before & after me)

3. Location of event (include specific room for my program, if known)

4. Occasion of event

5. Does the event have a theme or name?

6. Approximate number of attendees

7. How will the room be set-up? (Classroom style? Theater style? Banquet style?)

8. Will there be screen(s) set up for slides?

9. Age range of attendees

10. Gender ratio of attendees

11. Attire for the program

12. Where are attendees from?

13. How did they travel to event? Fly? Drive?

14. If the event is at a hotel, are most attendees staying there? Are any attendees staying there?

15. Are attendees bringing spouses, families, or guests to the event?

16. If so, will they be attending my program?

17. Will there be any children at my program?

18. Will attendees receive a "Welcome" bag? If so, what will be in it ?

19. Is there a t-shirt being given out or sold for the event?

20. If not, is there a t-shirt or golf shirt available that has the group's logo on it?

21. Is there a trade show as part of this event?

22. Who are the other speakers on the agenda for the entire event?

23. Who will be introducing me and what is their title?

24. What are the job titles and/or responsibilities of the attendees?

25. How often do these attendees get together for this kind of meeting/event?

26. Do most of the attendees know each other?

27. If not, do *any* of the attendees know each other?

28. Should I be aware of any potential hecklers or "difficult" audience members?

29. Can we review all of my audio-visual needs?

30. What time can I do a sound check for the event?

PART 2 — QUESTIONS ABOUT GROUP

Please send me internet links (or hard copies) of any websites, promotional literature, newsletters (internal & external), organizational chart, employee or organization handbooks, annual reports, basically EVERYTHING that you can get your hands on that has anything to do with the group.

1. Name of the group

2. Are they part of a larger organization or parent company?

3. Website(s) for the group

4. Any industry websites to study

5. Buzzwords, lingo, acronyms, jargon, etc. associated with your group or industry

6. General info if the group is a *business*: locations, number of employees, organizational structure, mission statement, products, services, history, etc.

7. General info if the group is an *association*: number of members, leadership & staff structure, criteria for membership, professional designations, awards, meetings schedules, history, etc.

8. Is there a software program or computer system or intranet that is specific to your group? If several, which is the most frustrating to use?

9. Major competitors (and their weaknesses)

10. Any regulatory or compliance organizations that cause stress

11. Other industries/professions/groups that are *not* liked by attendees

12. Recent (or not so recent) successes or initiatives

13. Recent (or not so recent) projects or initiatives that did *not* work

14. Recent awards/honors/accolades

15. Sensitive subjects—what do avoid

16. Hot buttons/pet peeves of employees/members

17. Hot buttons/pet peeves of management/officers

18. Hot buttons/pet peeves of customers/clients

19. Attendees' main obstacles/hurdles/hassles/what keeps them up at night

20. What are some of the difficult tasks or responsibilities that attendees face on a regular basis?

21. Any former employees /members /industry people to poke fun at?

22. Are there any high-profile employees, managers, officers, members, attendees, etc.—basically your group's well-known people—that I can mention? What are their names, titles, sayings, personality traits, habits, things they are known for?

23. Tell me about a *great* day at work. What would that look like?

24. Tell me about a *terrible* day at work. What would that look like?

25. If attendees are all from the same geographic area, is there something about that area that it's known for? Is there anything going on in the area currently that is a topic of conversation?

26. Is there anything memorable that happened at this event in recent years?

27. What is your main objective for this meeting or event?

28. What is your main objective for *my* program at this event?

29. Are there any specific messages or themes you want conveyed, directly or indirectly, during my presentation?

30. Is there anything I *haven't* asked you that I should be aware of?

67

Customized parody book covers

THIS IS ONE OF THE EASIEST WAYS TO GET BIG LAUGHS from a customized joke. Basically, you are taking a popular book, and graphically changing the title to something funny about the group you are speaking to.

For example, your research tells you that a certain task is difficult for the employees of a company. For the purposes of this example, we'll say that it is "processing refunds from the Phoenix office." You could then doctor up a cover of one of the many " ...... For Dummies" books to read "Processing Refunds From Phoenix For Dummies."

You can make the new cover by scanning the existing cover, and then playing around with the fonts to match a similar typeface to substitute the new word(s). You then print out the new cover and paste it on the existing cover. This gives you what appears to be a genuine book, which you can hold up and get your laugh.

If you are "graphically challenged" on the computer, a graphic designer can easily create a funny cover for you for a small amount of money (If you have no idea what a "scanner" or a "font" is, then you are also "computer challenged" and will definitely need to call the graphic designer.)

If you are presenting to a larger group—or you just don't want to mess with the hassle of pasting the new cover on the book—you can easily just show the parody cover on a slide. Holding up a "real" book gets a bigger laugh, but showing the parody book on a slide also works well—and is much easier.

When giving your presentation, you can set up the joke by saying, "1 know that there are some great difficulties with processing refunds out of Phoenix. That's why this new book is available *(at which point you would hold up the book)*—'Processing Refunds From Phoenix For Dummies'."

Another great title to parody is the "Chicken Soup For The Soul" books. For example, if your research tells you that a certain committee doesn't feel they're getting enough attention, you can create a cover that says "Chicken Soup For The Holiday Committee's Soul."

You would then set up the joke by saying, "You know, the holiday committee just doesn't get enough recognition for the work they do. That's why there's a new book that's been published that documents all the heart-warming work they accomplish—'Chicken Soup For The Holiday Committee's Soul'."

The key to making a parody of the "Dummies" or "Chicken Soup" covers is that you must create a new title that's extremely specific to the group. If it's too generic, there's a good chance that there's already a "Dummies" or "Chicken Soup" book with that title! You need to come up with a title that would *never* be a real book title for a mass market.

I'm often asked about the legalities of producing these parody book covers. My research tells me that because you are simply displaying the book covers in a presentation for the purposes of parody and satire, you are not risking copyright infringement.

However, if you were to *sell* a parody book with that cover, that's a different situation that might require permission. But if you simply display them for the purposes of parody or satire, you're probably fine. It's no different than when the late-night talk show hosts do similar bits with a whole array of phony book covers. They don't get permission for their parodies, and you likely won't have to either.

Please know, though, I am not *an attorney and this is* not *legal advice. If you have any questions or concerns on this matter, you should definitely consult with your own lawyer.*

The "Dummies" and "Chicken Soup" books are some of the easiest ones to create parody titles for, but they're not the only ones. I've also used ones like "Green Eggs & Ham" (which became "Green Eggs and Cam"—a real estate term) and "Who Moved My Cheese?" (which became "Who Moved My Chair?" for an entire office being reorganized).

In order to get the maximum laughs from this bit, the books you select to parody must be very well-known and popular books. The examples I've used are book titles that were still popular at the time of this book's publication.

But if you've never heard of "Dummies" or "Chicken Soup" books, chances are you're reading this many years later and there are a whole array of *new* popular book titles that are ripe for parody. Go for it!

(And if you *are* reading this many years later, that means either my book has been very successful....or else this is a *very* old copy!)

68

Customized parody phone menu scripts

YOUR RESEARCH WILL HOPEFULLY TELL YOU THE different "hot buttons" of the audience. You can then write a phone menu script, where each of the "hot buttons" becomes one of the menu choices for the caller.

You set up the bit by saying "the group is well aware of its problems and is even going as far to address them directly on the new phone system. Now when you call the group's phone number, you hear this" and then you either read the script yourself live or have it pre-taped to play.

An example of the script might be: "Thank you for calling the Acme Widget Company. If you're calling because your shipment is six weeks late, please press 1. If you're calling because your assembly instructions are written in Sudanese, please press 2. If you're calling because our website doesn't work, please press 3. If you're calling because you want to sue us, get in line."

If you decide to read the script live, put the microphone as close to your mouth as possible, to achieve that "announcer"-like sound.

If you decide to have the script recorded and played back, you might want to have someone of the opposite sex record it, so that there is a change in dynamics to what the audience has been hearing.

If you decide to go the route of the pre-taped version, it need not be something elaborate. You can just record it on your phone—and then hold the phone up to the microphone at that point in the speech. Having the recording on the phone also serves the purpose of pretending you're actually calling the phone number.

My preference is to perform the script live. That gives you the ability to pause accordingly between laughs, edit something out if you need to, and even add something in spontaneously that might have been inspired by earlier events.

If the humor is intended for a client—and not your fellow employees—you want to be very cautious of which warts you expose in displaying "your company's sense of humor." The sample script above would not work well for a sales pitch—unless you said it was the phone menu from the *competition*. (See Tip #55 for how to poke fun at the competition.)

69

Change the words in an existing acronym

ONE OF THE EASIEST WAYS TO USE THIS TECHNIQUE is if the name of the group you're addressing is an acronym. You then come up with *new* words to replace the *existing* words in the acronym.

This technique can work very well if you're looking for a good opening line. l have found that over 70% of the groups with "acronym names" have an "A" as one of the letters.

Usually the "A" stands for "Association," but it's not important what it stands for. In our new version, the "A" now stands for "Amway." We then use the other letters to create the name of a group that would be selling Amway.

Here are some I've used:

DMA—Dealers Marketing Amway

NSA—Nutritionists Selling Amway

AAPA—American Affiliates Promoting Amway

FRSA—Florida Residents Selling Amway

NEDA—New Entrepreneurs Dealing Amway

SSRA—Seasoned Salespeople Retailing Amway

You get the idea. Almost any acronym with the letter "A" can be twisted into an Amway group. Now you begin by saying, "Ladies & gentlemen, I'm glad I found the room we're meeting in today. Did you know that there's *another* group meeting in this hotel called DMA. Dealers Marketing *Amway*. 1 bought $200 worth of stuff before I realized I was in the wrong room!"

Of course, if you're already using the opening in Tip #30 ("Under the pretense"), you wouldn't use this Amway reference, too. Pick one or the other. The first Amway reference will get a laugh. A second one will not.

(And like we discussed in Tip #30, if you *are* addressing an Amway group, you need to stay away from both of these tips.)

Changing the words in an acronym is not just limited to the names of associations. Most corporate audiences have an abundance of acronyms that they use on a daily basis. They often have acronyms for sales systems, ordering systems, computer programs, company divisions, employee titles, etc.

The best way to posture the humor is to say something like this, "We've had so many complaints with the TASCO program, it now stands for 'This Antiquated System Can't Operate'."

Or "I think that DSM now stands for 'Don't Seem Motivated'."

Turning these acronyms into new words is relatively easy. I typically will go through a spelling dictionary and study the list of words that begin with the first letter I'm trying to change my new word to. Once I find several options to work with, I write those down, and then do the same thing with each of the other letters. Eventually I come up with the combination of words that will work very well in tandem to create the biggest laugh possible.

70

Create an acronym
from a regular word

THIS TECHNIQUE IS SORT OF THE "ADVANCED VER-sion" of the previous tip. Here we are taking an actual word that is *not* an acronym—and making it one.

I usually have success with this one by using the name of the company I'm addressing. This only works for a one-word name. If you do it for a multi-word name, it becomes too long of a process for the audience to stay focused on, and too long to be "believable" that it could be an acronym.

Again, your pre-program research is the key to knowing what will be funny to your audience. Here are a few examples of ones I've used. The humor is very inside, and would only work for that specific audience. But, when it works, it works BIG!

EMPIRE-—Everyone Makes Promises; It's
Really Exhausting!
(Note: Empire is an insurance company)

LENNAR—-Looked Everywhere, Never Noticed
Any Renovations
(*Note: Lennar is a large home building company.*)

HALIFAX—Handling Aggravating Lengthy Internal Faxes
And Xeroxes
(*Note: Halifax is a hospital that was trying to become "paperless."*)

OMEGA—Opportunity Means Expanding
Gloria's Acquisitions
(*Note: Omega is a travel company that was growing at a rapid pace, owned by a woman named Gloria.*)

You set up the joke by saying, "I did some research and found out that the name Empire is actually an acronym.

E-M-P-I-R-E. Everyone Makes Promises; It's Really Exhausting." To make the joke work effectively, you must spell out the letters out loud first, and then announce the words that they stand for.

Like in the tip before, I find the easiest way to create these is by going through a spelling dictionary and jotting down the words that seem like they might work. Then, just like solving a crossword puzzle, you play with the words so that they make sense in a phrase or sentence.

The acronym can also take the form of two sentences, like the Empire example above. Or you can use a sentence followed by a one-word exclamation:

MCGRAW—Many Clients Get Really Annoyed. Wow!

The key for this tip to succeed is that it must flow easily when you say it out loud. (And, of course, the words need to form a thought that would be funny.)

The McGraw example is also an illustration that the acronym creation need not be limited to the company name. In this case, it was someone's last name. (Someone, albeit with a good sense of humor.)

The acronym bit will work for any high-profile word that the audience is familiar with, as long as you can create the funny words that the letters stand for.

If you have the creative urge, you can come up with several options for what the acronym is, and read them all. However, you should make sure the additional acronyms are on totally different topics than your first one, so as not to appear redundant.

Also, the law of diminishing returns suggests that you probably don't want to do more than three or four acronyms on any one word. No matter how funny they are, the novelty wears off, and the humor starts to appear thin.

Here's an example of some of the other options I used for Empire, after doing the first one:

Expecting Millennials' Panic, I.T. Really Expanded

Embarrassing Marketing Pieces Inhibit Real Excitement

Even McCartney Pays Insurance Rentals Elsewhere

Again, these mean nothing to you, but to the Empire audience they were hysterical! It never hurts to remind you again, as we learned mere pages ago in Tip #65, that the more *specific* the humor, the more *terrific* the humor!

Be willing to take the extra time to customize your humor with acronyms like these, and reap the benefits of big laughs from your audience.

71

Go for the typo!

MANY GROUPS HAVE A ONE-LINE SLOGAN OR CATCH phrase or advertising line they are known for. This can be mined for humor in the following way.

Let's say the company's slogan is "Together We're Better." You say, "We were supposed to have a big banner hanging behind me that showed your slogan 'Together We're Better'. Unfortunately, when we put it up this morning, we found there was a typo in it. It said, 'Together We're *Bitter*'. And that just sends the wrong message, doesn't it?"

Basically, you are changing one word in the slogan to a different one through this imaginary mistake, and giving an entirely new meaning to the slogan. Even though the banner is non-existent, the audience's imagination kicks in and they are able to visualize the errant banner.

Many meetings are deemed with a "theme," and the theme becomes ripe for the same kind of joke. "We were supposed to have a banner behind me with the theme of this meeting 'Our Teams Will Be More Visible.' Unfortunately, when we put it up this afternoon, there was a typo in it. It said, 'Our *Tears* Will Be More Visible.' Now, I know some of you are frustrated, but that just sends the wrong message, doesn't it?."

This bit won't work all of the time. You must have a slogan or meeting theme that lends itself to the "typo." Make sure that you research all of the group's promotional materials. There may be a secondary phrase they use that could work well for you.

To maximize the laugh, the "typo" should just be a one-letter mistake. If the mistake is a whole word—"Growing Our Way To The Top" becomes "Groaning Our Way To The Top"-—it's just not that clever and the bit will get a mild reaction, at best.

72

Quoting cartoon characters for philosophy

PICK UP A COPY OF BARTLETT'S QUOTATIONS OR Google "famous quotations" and you'll see quotes from authors, politicians, scientists, poets, philosophers, etc.

What you won't see are quotes from Fred Flintstone, Homer Simpson, Porky Pig, Scooby Doo, etc. And yet these are the quotes that can get you the biggest laughs. Why? Because they're so out of context. These are not names who typically get quoted in speeches, and yet they are more well known to your audience than the folks in the quote books.

Let's say you make an important point in your presentation. To follow that with, "And this is a point that most people agree with. I think it was that great American philosopher Fred Flintstone who said, 'Yabba dabba do'." And you must deliver the line very seriously, as though Mr. Flintstone's quote is a very important one.

Let all the other speakers quote Shakespeare. You can get laughs by emphasizing your point with, "And when faced with adversity, I think it was that great American philosopher Scooby Doo who said, 'Rut ro.'" Again, your laugh comes from saying the quote completely seriously.

This technique is also one that's best used sparingly. It will get laughs once or twice because of the surprise element, but beyond that it will lose its effectiveness and start to appear sophomoric.

73

You gotta have a gimmick!

ALMOST ALL OF THE TIPS WE'VE DISCUSSED UP TO now involve just you and your microphone. When all is said and done, it is what you *say* that will generate the majority of your laughs.

However, there are certain "extracurricular activities" you can engage in to add more laughs to your program. These require extra skill, time, budget, rehearsal, or a combination of all of the above. But when used in conjunction with your other humor techniques, these extras can gain you some great extra laughs:

Magic—you don't have to be David Copperfield with big illusions. Even some simple sleight-of-hand can add a great dimension to your talk.

Juggling—when they're not expecting it, this can dazzle the audience. It can be as simple as juggling three balls, because, really, how many in a typical audience can do that?

Dancing—this one is for the really brave! There's nothing funnier than seeing someone dance—in public—-by themselves. If you can shed your inhibitions, put on a well-known song and go for it! Even if it's only for a few seconds, perhaps, to make a point about "being confident" or "letting go of your fears" or whatever you use to justify it, the surprise element will get you big laughs.

Props—Even Carrot Top started with only a handful of small props. (I know, I was there.) A trip to any Spencer Gifts (in many major malls)—or a fun internet search—will yield a surprising array of items that can be used to add some additional humor to your presentation.

Costumes—The First-Cousin to Props! Some speakers have enormous success with having a costume hidden under their regular clothing. At a certain point in the presentation, they rip off their "normal" clothing to reveal their: Superman outfit, coach's uniform, bridal gown, adventurer's outfit, scientist's lab coat, etc.

The list is only as long as one's imagination. The costume serves to illustrate a point or theme you are trying to make. You can then finish out the program as the new character. Or you can put your regular clothes back on again over the costume at a certain point, if the logistics work, to conclude the talk.

The variation on this technique is to *begin* your presentation in the costume—and then take the costume off at some point to continue the program in your regular clothing.

Regardless of whether you begin in the costume—or end in the costume—there has to be a reason to justify *why* you're using the costume. As long as there's a reason (e.g.: a coach's uniform to talk to the attendees like they're a 'team'), the audience will "buy into" your use of the costume—and laugh at the surprise element.

Limericks—

"There once was a man from West Neechis.
Who lectured on the science of leeches.
He was boring as hell,
But began to do well,
By adding limericks like this to his speeches"

Yes, limericks are silly. But the audiences love that A-A-B-B-A rhyme pattern and will always laugh at a well-constructed limerick.

Audience participation games—There are scores of books written on these interactive gems. They are great ice-breakers or mid-afternoon-wake-up boosters that takes some of the pressure off of you.

Use your gimmicks sparingly. I wouldn't use more than two or three in a presentation, unless you're a professional entertainer. These gimmicks should be used to spice things up, but not necessarily as the essence of your program.

However, if you become really proficient at one of them, that gimmick can become your "signature" humor piece—the one you get known for—and the one that leaves the audience laughing every time.

There is one more gimmick I'd like to tell you about. This one is so good, it gets its own chapter. Turn the page!

74

Song parodies

THIS IS MY PERSONAL FAVORITE, AND THE GIMMICK I've used the most in my own programs. This is where you take the words of a popular song and change the words to something funny.

It's important for the song to be well-known, because if the audience doesn't know the original that you're parodying, much of the humor is lost.

Also, the closer you can keep the new parody lyrics to the original lyrics, the funnier the song will be.

You can just sing the song parody acapella (without any backing music). But it's *much* better if you're able to have live or pre-recorded music to play while you sing the new (funny) words you've written.

If you want to play the music live, you'll need to master either the guitar or piano. (I guess you could also use an accordion as your accompanying instrument, but your best bet is probably a keyboard or guitar.)

Even if you don't know how to play one of those instruments now, there's nothing that precludes you from learning it! You can learn the basics of playing a guitar or piano in less than six months. Actors learn new skills like this all the time for movie roles—there's no reason you can't either.

If you don't want to bother with playing a live instrument, you could simply play a background track of the song. A quick search of "Karaoke tracks" on-line will show you background tracks of pretty much every song ever recorded.

The upside of using Karaoke tracks is that they sound very close to the original song—which the audience finds very entertaining.

The downside to using Karaoke tracks is that they're usually longer than you want the parody to be. (Although you could always edit the track or turn it off early during your program—but neither of those are ideal.)

You're also locked into the tempo (speed) and the key (how high or low you need to sing). (Although some Karaoke websites allow you to change the key.)

Another option is to have a friend who plays guitar or piano record the song for you. It's not as full a sound as a Karaoke track, but you gain the advantage of having the song the exact length, tempo, and key that you want

There could probably be an entire book written on the art of song parodies, but here's my quick take on it.

- The song should be short—once the laugh has been generated due to the parody, the "thrill is gone" and the novelty wears off quickly. Nobody wants to sit through four verses and four choruses of a song parody. Almost all of the 1,300+ song parodies that I have written are less than 90 seconds.

- The song should be up-tempo. Words are much funnier when they're coming at you at a faster pace than if they are being sung slowly in a ballad.

- The song should have a simple music structure. This means that it should contain just a few chords, so that you're not bogged down with musical gymnastics.

If you're going to be using any music in your program that's *not* for parodies—perhaps for dancing or walk-on music—you'll need to make sure that the venue or the meeting planner has a license to play or perform music there.

Most meeting planners are aware of this, and many venues that host events have these licenses. (These are music performing licenses provided by ASCAP and BMI, the two leading music publishing groups.) With these in place, you are free to perform or play recorded songs in a live setting.

The ASCAP and BMI requirements are typically for non-parody songs. If you're doing song parodies, that is a "gray" area as to whether they are protected under the laws of parody and satire.

Most case law has sided with the parody performers, allowing them to perform the parody songs without having to get permission or pay the publisher. However, an intellectual property attorney can give you much better guidance on this than I can And you might recall from some of my earlier tips, I am not a lawyer, so any questions you have on these matters should be directed to your own attorney.

75

Record every presentation you make

IF YOU WANT TO GET REALLY GOOD AT GETTING laughs, you've got to treat the process seriously. One key way to do that is to record every presentation that you make. This gives you a learning tool far more valuable than any book you can read.

When you listen to the recording afterwards, you hear exactly what resonated with the audience and what didn't. Some lines that you thought were outstanding might get little or no reaction, whereas other lines that were just filler end up getting a huge roar. But you can't rely on your memory—you're too caught up (or should be) in the delivery of the material—-and will only remember peripherally what happened.

The audience doesn't have to know you're recording the program. You can use your phone or there are small recorders that can fit easily into a pocket. Whichever recording device you use, you'll want to experiment with the microphone on it, to make sure that it can pick up both you *and* the audience.

You can also place the phone or recorder on a table on the stage, or on the lectern, or even on a chair in the front of the room.

If you don't mind the audience seeing it, you can even gain some extra laughs from its presence. If a line falls flat, you can pick up the recorder and say directly into it, "Note to self. Never use that line again." And the opposite—if a line goes over very well, with an extended reaction—you can pick up the recorder and say directly into it, "Note to self, that line works well."

But the main reason you're recording the program is for you to review it afterwards. And the sooner you can review it, the better. Try not to let more than 24 hours go by between the presentation and your review of it. At the very least, try to review the talk before you give your next one, so that you don't make the same mistakes twice.

Some humor coaches recommend videotaping every presentation, and that can be very valuable if it's practical for you to do so. But a video camera—even if it's just your phone on a tripod—can sometimes be intimidating to an audience and might inhibit their laughter. They're wondering, "Why is this being taped?"

Also, reviewing a video requires you to sit in front of a screen for the length of the speech, which might not always be practical to do. Reviewing an audio version of your program can be done in the car or while doing something else. However, if you speak regularly, you should try to videotape yourself at least once every 20 speeches for your own review.

In addition to recording every program, l also keep a log of the material l used for each speech. Again, I do this for a living, so it's important for me not to do the exact same material to the exact same crowd. You may not be speaking that often, but you still could be well served by keeping a written record of the humor you use.

It could be anything from a simple hand-written loose-leaf notebook to a well-structured computer database. It should be something that's easy for you to fill out and easy for you to reference. if nothing else, it will serve as a great historical record for your grandchildren of your quest for laughter from the masses.

76

Be ready to "be funny" on a moment's notice

PERHAPS YOU PURCHASED THIS BOOK SO THAT YOU'D have a resource to use the next time you're asked to give a speech or make a presentation. Well, you never know when you may have to give that speech *RIGHT NOW*.

Part of your preparation for being funny in front of an audience should be treated as though it might be necessary for you to do iit today—because it just might be! You never know when the person who was scheduled to address the volunteers, the person who was supposed to present the award, or the person who was going to speak at the meeting is suddenly not available. You may be the person they now turn to, to rise to the occasion.

There are many tips in this book that can get you instant laughs. Go through the book and make a note of the ones you could use right now, in front of any audience. Keep them on a small slip of paper in your wallet or your purse and review it often.

Most readers will know the audience they might be asked to address on a moment's notice, and can easily prepare some material to have ready for that occasion. Even if it's a crowd you don't know at all, there's plenty of generic material you can use, and get some easy, early laughs.

Most of you will work hard at preparing humor when you know the date on the calendar for your presentation is approaching. I'm suggesting that you work hard on preparing humor, even when there is no date for you to speak on the calendar at all.

Sometimes in life, opportunities present themselves in strange ways. The opportunity to stand in front of an audience—and make them laugh—is one of the most valuable experiences a person can have.

The power of humor is second to none, and you should be well-prepared to use that power should that opportunity fall into your lap. Trust me, you'll thank me later. (And, conversely, if you *don't* have some humor ready in your back pocket at all times—and you get called on to step up to the microphone—you'll curse yourself that you didn't follow this advice!)

77

From the page to the stage

WELL, HERE WE ARE AT THE END OF THE BOOK.

Are you ready to try everything you've learned?

Are you ready to try *anything* you've learned?

It will do you *no* good to have had read this book—and gotten excited about the possibility of using some of the tips in here—and then do nothing about it. You must now take the tips from the page to the stage!

You probably won't want to try too much humor at once. You're bound to get overwhelmed or confused, and that could easily lead to discouragement. Instead, you should select three of your favorite tips and try those first.

Really work those tips.

Rewrite the words if necessary.

Practice your delivery.

Become confident.

And then work those three tips into your next presentation. Hopefully, you'll get big laughs, which will form the foundation for trying three *more* tips the next time, and so on. (Note: You don't have to do three tips. If this is all a little daunting to you, you can try *one* tip at a time. And if you feel that you can handle these tips with ease, go ahead and work in a dozen at a time!)

And while you're at the end of the book, you're really at the beginning of your humor journey. You took the initial step of buying the book, which shows you're serious about getting laughs. Now it's time to reap the rewards of the book.

If you're not being asked to make presentations on any kind of regular basis, seek out opportunities to address an audience. I don't mean the folks waiting at the bus station, but there are ways to put yourself in a position to be speaking to crowds.

Volunteer to do training at work. If you're at a social function, and it's appropriate, propose a toast.

Join a committee of a local civic group and work your way into a position to run the meetings.

Or simply join your local Toastmasters club, where you can speak to your fellow members on a regular basis. Toastmasters is a great training vehicle for your speaking, but you should also be seeking out genuine speaking opportunities, where the audience is "real."

The more you speak, the more you will become comfortable in adding humor to every presentation you do. And the better you will become at getting laughs from any audience.

Now go out there and get some big laughs. You're gonna love every minute of it! And your audiences will love *you* for giving them the gift of laughter!

If you'd like individual help in adding humor to your presentation, David Glickman is available to be your own personal Laughter Crafter.

Visit www.FunnierSpeeches.com to learn more about how David can punch up any presentation with customized, relevant, and appropriate humor—specifically for your audience.

David can also be reached via e-mail at David@ DavidGlickman.com.